GETTING YOUR JOB
God's Way

BUNMI LARA OLUSANYA

SYNCTERFACE

Syncterface Media
London
www.syncterfacemedia.com

GETTING YOUR JOB GOD'S WAY
ISBN: 978-0-9933860-7-7

Copyright. © February 2018 BUNMI LARA OLUSANYA
All Rights Reserved

Published in the United Kingdom by

Syncterface Media
London

www.syncterfacemedia.com
info@syncterfacemedia.com

Cover Design:
Syncterface Media

ACKNOWLEDGEMENTS

First and foremost, I acknowledge God the father, the son and Holy Spirit for being my help and strength.

I will like to thank my family members for their help, support and encouragement especially Danielle for helping with the editing of the book.

Thanks Danielle, I couldn't have done it without you.

DEDICATION

To my mother,

Mrs Rebecca Ayodele Longe,

A strong woman who taught me how to be a fighter.

Contents

A WORD FROM THE AUTHOR

*T*he world is becoming a more and more competitive place to live in. From an early age, parents are ensuring that their children are given an edge over their peers. Children as young as two or three years old need to go through screening processes before gaining admission into private schools. This demand for high performance does not stop with admission. Many of these children also get personal tutors in a bid to guarantee outcomes. It is not uncommon to find children who are fluent in multiple languages or eight-year olds writing computer programs. The genius of yesterday is truly becoming the norm of today.

Despite great efforts made to prepare candidates for the future, it seems that getting a job is all but guaranteed. In an increasingly global pool of candidates, where information and technology is ever changing, the need to remain competitive has never been more significant. Even the best of the best struggle to find jobs in this environment where constantly raising the bar is the norm.

Doing your research, presenting yourself and your resume to distinguish yourself from other candidates are amongst the things you should do to get a job but what do you do when your best appears not to be good enough? What do you do when it seems you have been eliminated from the contest even before you begin?

This book will tell you how to get your job God's way.

Although I have always focused on the spiritual to get a job, it would be remiss of me not to mention practical, natural steps that need to be taken get a job.

Invest in training yourself to update current skills or acquire new ones. There are many free training resources on platforms like *YouTube*. If you have no commercial experience, volunteer to work for free to gain relevant experience.

Where possible, get a professional to assist with your resume. Your resume needs to stand out. Register on platforms like *LinkedIn* where your resume can be discovered. Attend networking events and don't despise friends and former colleagues.

Write a professional cover letter and apply for jobs that are good matches for your skills and experience. When the interview openings start coming, research about the company you are interviewing with and prepare extensively for your interview. Find out the format of the Interview. Some interviews have technical tests, group discussions and presentations. Be prepared.

Map out your route to the interview before the day. Dress professionally, arrive early and sell yourself during the interview process.

My prayer is that God will speak to you through this book and despite any of your shortcomings, get you your desired job.

Bunmi Lara Olusanya

PART I

Laying the foundation

CHAPTER 1

SHATTERED DREAMS

Whilst sitting down on a red double-decker bus with tears streaming down my cheeks, I wiped the tears with the back of my hand so no one would notice. All I could think of was the song "Shattered dreams, Shattered dreams, nothing I tried turned out right[1]".

Overwhelmed by many "I regret to inform you" letters and with no job in sight, I saw no light at the end of the tunnel. After all, I was a Christian and had prayed. I had acted out in faith but wondered why I had door after door shut in my face. Why couldn't I get a job? Was I asking for too much?

Though British by birth, I graduated from a Nigerian University and went back to England expecting to get a job in my field of expertise. I thought it would be a walk in the park. Little did I know that I had just landed into a pool of extremely qualified immigrants of African descent working in menial jobs to get the highly coveted "British Experience." My previous experience in a foreign country was not good

---

[1] Mary Mckee and The Genesis

enough. "British Experience" was required. But how was I expected to get the type of job I sought if no one was willing to give me the opportunity?

The first breakthrough I had was when I got a job as a Senior Clerk. It was not the type of job I was looking for, but it at least got me working in an office environment. Most of the people I knew were still doing menial jobs, so I felt good compared to them until my contract ended and I was thrown back into the pool. I had nowhere and no one to turn to but God.

It was during this period of my life that I got hold of a message from a man of God that I listened to over and over again. This message changed my life and my walk with God. Although my situation did not change externally, there was an internal change taking place. I was feeding my spirit with the word of God, and this word was transforming me from the inside out. In addition to listening to this message, I spent a lot of time praying in the spirit.

The message I was listening to taught me that I did not need anybody to prophesy to me nor did I need to look around for prophecies from God. All I needed to do was to rely on the word of God in the Bible. The word of God was a more sure word of prophecy (2 Peter 1:19). It also encouraged me to believe that I could build my entire life on the word of God, which could never fail.

I listened to this message nearly every day for

almost a year, at the end of which I decided to pursue a master's degree in information technology.

During this master's program, a role became available in the Career's Advisory Centre of the university which I was attending, and I decided to apply for it. The interview process was such that candidates had to call to confirm attendance. However, due to my workload, I realised that I could not attend the interview and decided not to place the required confirmation call.

The evening before the interview, I got a call from the director of the centre who, apparently impressed, with my application, asked why I had not confirmed my attendance. His call prompted me to rearrange my schedule and attend the interview. I attended, and I got the job. This particular job was instrumental in me getting my first commercial IT experience.

While working at this position, I got a call from an organisation looking to employ a student for a short term contract. This brought a glimmer of hope. The job specification looked interesting and attractive to me. I even considered sneakily applying as the sole applicant but thank God, my better judgement prevailed. I mentioned it to my boss, placed the advert on the notice board and, of course, did not forget to apply for the role. Had I not been working at the Centre at the time, I most likely would have missed the opportunity. The coincidences did not stop there.

A few months after, I was on the short-list for interviews.

On the day of the interview, I arrived at Hyde Park Station in London and was trying to locate the office when I saw a man walking down the road, dressed in a suit and brushing his hair. I asked for directions, and he turned out to be the director of the hiring department. I was going to have to see him after my interview with the hiring manager. What a coincidence!

The hiring manager kept the questions coming, and I answered as best as I could. She asked if I had certain skills in a particular area which I did not have. She told me not to worry that she did not have those skills either. The interview ended, and to my surprise a few weeks later, I was offered the job. My first IT experience in London was about to begin. I had secured a job without knowing anyone or having any experience in the industry. God went before me and made room for me. I was one of the few from my class who got a job almost immediately after completing the master's program. This, a few years earlier, would have been next to impossible. Something about this situation was different compared to the previous opportunities I had explored without success. God had intervened and helped me get my first commercial experience without having to lie or know anyone in the industry.

Many years have gone past, and I can attest to God helping me time and time again and taking

me through hurdles that I would otherwise have
been unable to cross.

CHAPTER 2

YOUR DESIRE - WHAT DO YOU WANT?

*S*ince you have picked up this book, I am assuming that you are either looking for a job or working at a job that you are not satisfied with. You might have tried many things without much success. I can assure you that by coming to God for help, you have done the right thing. However, you have to come to God the right way. You need to have a clear idea of what you want before approaching God. What type of job do you want? You might say, "Well, I want to see what is out there first before I apply" or "I don't care, I just want to be able to pay my bills."

However, if you want to approach God with a request, you must at least have an idea of what you want before you approach him. For instance, if you want to get a loan from the bank, you don't just go to the bank and say "I want a loan". Saying that you want a loan will not automatically qualify you for one. You need to be a bit more specific about what type of loan you want. Questions that the bank authorities may ask you include "What type of loan do you want?"; "How much do you want to borrow?"; "Over how many years are you willing to repay the loan?"; and "What do you need the loan for?", amongst others. By doing so, they will be able to assess whether or not they should lend you the money. Similarly, you need to tell God what exactly you want in a job. Don't just go to God saying that you want a job. Spell out what type of job you are looking for.

Before you go to God in prayer with your request for a job, you need to be very clear about the kind of job you want. I have listed a few pointers that would help you spell out what you want in a job.

Before I do that, I would like to ask you a quick leading question. If you knew the president of this country and they said to you, "You can have whatever job you want. I give you an hour to write the type of job you want on a sheet of paper and I will see to it that you get the job you have requested for." What would you write on that sheet of paper? This exercise should help you decide what to write about what you want to ask God for in a job.

Well, you may say, "He is God, he can give me whatever job he wants to give me." However, he wants you to ask for something specific so that when you get it, there will be no doubt in your mind that it was God who helped you. You will not just think it happened by coincidence. You will be sure that because you asked God for a job, he heard you and he answered.

So many people ask God for things, and when he

fulfils their wishes, they get a bit confused and think that maybe it wasn't God who helped them or that maybe it just happened by coincidence. God wants you to be sure that he is the one who has answered your prayers; so, he wants you to have a very clear (and not at all vague) request of what you want.

Another thing to bear in mind when writing out your request is that although we can ask God for anything, we need to ask him for what we can believe him for or exercise our faith for. For example, if you have £5 and you go to a restaurant, it would be unwise for you to order food worth £100 when you know that you do not have enough money to pay for it.

Likewise, you need to pray for what your faith can handle. In short, do not overstretch your faith. Someone that has never used their faith for a headache would be silly to try to exercise their faith for an eye that is going blind. It might be better for them to believe God that a Doctor would be able to perform surgery to correct their eyes successfully.

Since we are not going to use God's faith to get what we want, we need to be honest and start where we are in our faith walk. Or better still, we can work on increasing our faith. The Bible says that "Faith comes by hearing, and hearing by the word of God. (*Romans 10:17*)" What I am trying to say is that God can do anything, but what can you believe him for? Our faith is the currency that we are going to use to get what we want from God. We can only get from God what our currency of faith can buy. Do not write what you cannot believe for or what you don't need. If you are willing to accept a job that will take you an hour and a half to commute to, then do not write that you want a job that is five minutes away from home. You need to be honest about what you will or will not accept. For instance, if you write that you want a job that is five minutes away from home and two days after you write your request, an agent calls you for a job that is one and a half hours away from home, will you still go to the interview? If you are able to do this, then write that you would like a job that will not take you more than one and a half hours one way or even two hours one way. Personally, I always write that I do not want a job that will take me more than two hours to get to. Despite writing this, God has still been able to provide me with jobs that only took me 30 minutes door to door. Also, working in a city different from the city that I lived in was never an option for me because I had school-aged children. So, I never entertained an interview for a job that would take me away from the city I lived in. God has always been faithful in providing me with jobs in the location of my choice.

Just as job advertisements are always clear about the type of person they want, we need to be clear about the type of job that we want.

I don't believe that anybody wants to work for free. We need money to live daily, so a good remuneration is one of the most important things we look for in a job. If you write that you want a job that would pay a minimum of £20 an hour and you get offered a job that pays £15 an hour, will you accept it? If you will, then write that you want a job with a minimum of £15 an hour.

Furthermore, be realistic with your expectations. If you have just finished your first degree, it is seemingly unrealistic to expect to become the director of a company that you are applying to. Apply for the position that is commensurate with your qualifications/skills. If you are convinced that you have what it takes to apply for a higher position than that warranted by your qualification, then go with your convictions; but, never despise the days of humble beginnings (*Zechariah 4:10*). You need to start from somewhere.

The key here is to write what you can believe God for. Remember that you need faith and patience to get your job.

> *12 That ye be not slothful, but followers of them who through faith and patience inherit the promises.*
>
> Hebrews 6:12 (KJV)

> *12 We do not want you to become lazy, but to imitate those who through faith and patience inherit what has been promised.*
>
> Hebrews 6:12 (NIV)

You may ask, "What has faith got to do with writing out my job desires?"

Faith is the currency that is going to bring your job from the spiritual realm into the natural one. You will get your job from God by applying your faith to his promises and waiting till the job manifests from the spiritual realm to the natural realm. That is why it is important to write down exactly what you mean and can believe for.

What do I write on the list? My suggestion is that you try to cover the areas that are most important to you in specific terms.

Relationship with God

I always like to write that I want a job that will not disturb my relationship with God. What is the use of getting a job that takes up all your time and will not allow you to attend Church, pray or spend time with God? I say this because a job that leaves no room for God cannot be from God because God wants us to spend time with him. We need him to lead, guide and direct us in this journey of life and he cannot do this if we do not have time daily to establish our fellowship with him. I must emphasize on the word "daily" here and not just spend a few hours with him on Sunday.

Salary

Another thing I like to write is the minimum

salary or salary range I desire. Writing down a minimum is better because by writing down a maximum, you are putting a cap on what you want from God.

Skills

It is also important to mention the skills you want to work with or the trade you would like to work in. If you would like a job in the medical field, then write that. If you want to work in the legal field, mention that. If you are an I.T. professional, then you would want to mention the technical skills that you would like to use or those you are looking to gain. For example, I cannot stand the sight of blood, so I would never accept a job to work as a nurse or a doctor (besides the fact that I do not have any medical qualification and so, would not even veer in that direction).

Boss/Supervisor

The type of boss I would like to work with is also something I like to put on my list. If you have worked with an unbearable boss, you will know the importance of putting this on your list. Likewise, if you work with someone that you get along with, that is one less thing to worry about. We spend most of our time at work, so it is important that we get along with those that we work with. Our superiors and subordinates should be people we can relate to.

Benefits and perks

This category is one a lot of people don't pay attention to, yet some of these could come in handy. Depending on your personal lifestyle, many organisations have benefits and perks which may include vouchers for after-school clubs, discounts on flight tickets, generous pension schemes, free loans on travel cards, free medical expenses, paid holidays, overtime, sickness benefits, time off for study, payment towards professional exams, life insurance cover, dental cover for the family, company cars, free gym memberships, free massages and stress relieve sessions, subsidized lunches in the staff canteen, among other things.

Some of these are nice to have. It is important that you mention those that would absolutely be important to you or list those that would just be nice to have. It might be unwise to turn down a job because they do not offer free stress relief sessions; however, if that is something that is important to you, then you will want to put that on your list.

Permanent or contract job

Some people prefer less risky jobs and would prefer the security of a permanent or full-time job. If that is you, then you should ask God for a permanent or full-time job. On the other hand, if you are a risk taker and are not bothered if you are out of work for a few months, then a contract-based or temporary job (that pays more but is for a fixed period of time) might suit you better. On the other hand, if you do not mind either, then state that as well.

Managerial / Supervisory roles / Future job prospects

Getting into management or staying as a team player should be something you put on your list. Some people think long term and look out for jobs with prospects for the future. This too can be added to your list.

Convenience for school runs

In the U.K., parents do not have the luxury of school buses like people in North America. As a working mother, I always wanted a job that would allow me to drop off my children in the morning. In the evenings, I used nannies, au pairs, or drop off services. Being able to find someone to pick my children in the evening was important to me, whereas, it was not an issue in the mornings. So, if this aspect is important to you, it is wise to put it on your list when writing out what you want in a job from God. There is no use getting a job and then deciding, after two weeks, that you cannot do it because you have childcare issues.

To summarize, these are a few of the things you might want to put down on your list. Please bear in mind that this list is not exhaustive. There are other issues/situations that might be peculiar to you that should definitely go on your list.

These issues could include the following:

- *The type of job;*
- *The type of skills you would like to use on your job;*
- *Type of boss you want – friendly and easy to get along with;*
- *Type of colleagues – friendly and easy to get along with;*
- *The maximum distance to work;*
- *The minimum salary that you would accept;*
- *Job perks;*
- *Your role as a supervisor/manager/ team player;*
- *Job prospects;*
- *Type of organization;*
- *Team size; and*
- *Special conditions, i.e. a job that would not hurt your relationship with God.*

After you have written your request, review it and see if you can visualize what you want to ask God for in a job.

CHAPTER 3

LAY A SOLID FOUNDATION BY FAITH BEFORE PRAYING

*N*ow that you've written down your desires, you need to build up your faith in God's word to ensure that it can withstand the test of time. Ninety-nine percent of the time, your job will not manifest the minute you pray for it. In fact, your situation might start looking worse after you pray. That is because the devil will throw everything at you to get you to doubt that you have your job. It is a good idea, therefore, to lay a solid foundation before you pray for what you desire.

What is faith?

> *¹Now faith is the substance of things hoped for, the evidence of things not seen.*
>
> *Hebrews 11:1 (KJV)*
>
> *¹Now faith is being sure of what we hope for, being convinced of what we do not see.*
>
> *Hebrews 11:1 (NET)*
>
> *¹Now faith is a well-grounded assurance of that which we hope and a conviction of the reality of things which we do not see.*
>
> *Hebrews 11:1 (WNT)*

Faith is taking God's word at face value amidst

contrary evidence. You need to have a scripture verse from the Bible that you will use as your foundation for approaching God. For instance, if someone has not promised you something, you have no basis for approaching them for help. On the other hand, if you have a document that shows that they have promised you something, you can approach them on the ground of that document and request for what they have promised. That is the same way in which you need to approach God with His word. The scripture verse that you approach God with, is what we term as the word from God on which you are standing.

You must have faith in that word from God which could either be from the Bible or from a word that God has spoken to you through someone. It is not right for you to say, "I know God can do everything and I believe he will give me a job." You need to have a chapter and verse from the Bible that you are standing on. That word from God is what you will need to hold onto till the job manifests in the physical realm. That particular word from God may be the only evidence that you will have to depend on till your job manifests. It will be your anchor against doubt and unbelief.

25But that which you have already hold fast till I come.

Revelation 2:25

Without any physical evidence to confirm the existence of the job, you will need to hold on to something till the job manifests. The statement from *Hebrews 11:1* quoted above states that faith is the substance of what we hope for. Hope is not tangible. You cannot touch or feel hope. Faith in the word of God, however, is what gives our hope tangibility. The word of God is the anchor that we will have to hold onto till the job actually becomes tangible or till the job actually manifests.

You will not get your job God's way if you are not prepared to hold onto and believe God's word in the face of joblessness and unemployment. Most of the time, there will be a waiting period between the time we pray and the time our job actually manifests. Laying a good foundation, and being rooted in and grounded on the scripture you are standing on is what will keep you from wavering during the waiting period.

On one of the occasions when I was believing God for a job, I took my time to carefully meditate on the following:

> *⁶But without faith, it is impossible to please him (God); for he that cometh to God must believe that he is, and that he is a rewarder of them that diligently seek him.*
>
> *Hebrews 11:6*

According to Dictionary.com, the word "impossible" means "*unable to be done, incapable of being done, difficult, hopelessly unsuitable, hardly possible and impracticable*".

Just as it is impossible for a dog to give birth to a cat, it is impossible for God to be pleased with us if we do not have faith. Stating the obvious, it is impossible for a dog to give birth to a cat. Due to genetics, a dog can only give birth to a puppy. In the same vein, if we do not have faith, we will not be able to please God, and if we do not please God, we will not get what we want from him.

God still loves us, but he will not be able to help us because we will not be coming to him the way he expects us to. There is a difference between God's love and God's provision. His love for us is unconditional, but his provisions are conditional.

Hebrews 11:6 says, "*Without Faith, it is impossible to please God, he that cometh to God must believe that he is, and that he is a rewarder of them that diligently seek him ...*"

If you decide that you want God to help you get a job, then you must believe. It is mandatory that if you approach God for help regarding your job; you must come believing. You cannot come hoping, wishing or pleading. You must come only one way, and that is to come believing God. What do you have to believe? You must believe that he is. Believe that he is what? Believe that he is the answer to whatever you are coming to him for. So, if you have come to him for a job, then you must believe that he is going to provide you with one. You must believe that he is the answer to your unemployment. You must believe that he is the answer to your joblessness. You must believe that He can get you exactly what you want – not "maybe", "comme ci, comme ca", "so, so" or "perhaps". You need to know certainly that He is, and that He is a rewarder of those who diligently seek him. When you come to God by faith, and you hold on to the word that you get from God, you will be rewarded. When you come to God for a job, you need to seek him diligently and not half-heartedly. You need to seek him by putting all your eggs in His basket.

Seeking God diligently means to be constant in your effort to accomplish something – to be attentive and persistent in doing something. It means to pursue something with persevering attention.

How long do you have to be diligent for? You should be diligent till the job manifests.

What if it takes a year before the job manifests? You will still need to be diligent. You will need to be constant. The velocity and tenacity with which you started your quest should not rise and fall because of what you see or do not see.

You need to remember that God cannot lie. If he says that he will give you a job, he will do so because He is able to do exceeding and abundantly above all that you can ever ask for or think of asking *(Ephesians 1:19)*.

Once you have got to the point where you are confident that the scripture you are standing on has sunk into your spirit and that you have more than just a 'mental assent' or mental acknowledgement of the scripture, then you are in a position to pray.

I always believe that I have got to this point when I do not have to think, but speak with a conviction from my heart that I have the job even though my senses may be telling me otherwise.

CHAPTER 4

STANDING ON THE WORD OF GOD

*N*ow that we've established that laying a solid foundation is important, how do I know the scripture to stand on? "Standing on the word" is a phrase that gets thrown around a lot when faced with a situation or challenge. But what exactly does it mean? It simply means looking for scriptural references for what you are reaching out to God for. There is no hard and fast rule about which bible verse or chapter to stand on.

There are so many ways scriptures can come to you to create the experience of you hearing from God. It's like the experience of a mobile phone picking up signals from a transmitter. There may be different transmitters between where you start your journey and your final destination. In order not to break connectivity with the person you are speaking to, the phone has to hop from transmitter to transmitter. Let us look at some examples of "transmitters" you may have along the way.

1. *A scripture someone else stood on*

   You hear someone share a testimony about how they got a job. They mention that they stood on a particular bible verse. That verse can be your starting point. Write down the scripture verse and use that as your own basis for trusting in God. Take the time to mull over this scripture till you are convinced that it is real. You need to realise that acting on God's word is not a formula. For instance, someone says, "*The Bible says God shall supply my needs, I trusted God with that verse and I got a job.*" You too can then take that bible verse and mull over it till you are convinced that God will supply your need for a job.

2. *Look up verses in the Bible*

You can look up verses on God's provision and use those as your starting point or you could also use a bible verse that ministered to you in Church.

3. *A bible verse quoted by the pastor*

Sometimes, the pastor may even be preaching on a totally different topic, but while he is preaching, a particular verse stands out to you. That verse should be one of the verses that you meditate on for your job.

4. *A scripture verse used in a Christian song*

You could be listening to Christian music, and the words from the song could literally just stand out. This happened to me once.

The words from the song "*Be magnified O Lord, you are highly exalted, and there is nothing you can't do, O Lord, my eyes are on you, Be magnified, O Lord, Be magnified*", ministered to me that God can do anything and that I had actually been believing in the lies that the enemy had been selling to me. I took this instance as God speaking to me, knowing that there was nothing he could not do and again, I got the job I believed him for.

5. *A scripture verse that stands out while you are reading the bible*

A verse may stand out to you whilst you are reading the bible, a Christian book or a magazine. That may just be the verse you need to use while believing for your job. You need to go over it, meditate on it and take your time to study it till it sinks into your spirit.

I was once going for a job interview. I had a one-year bible at that time, which listed the verses one had to read for every day of the year. While reading the scriptures allocated for that day, one verse stood out from all the others. It was *Exodus 23:20* which reads as follows:

> *[20]Behold, I send an Angel before thee, to keep thee in the way, and to bring thee into the place which I have prepared.*

> *Exodus 23:20*

I fixed my eyes on this verse and began to meditate on it. It was as if God was actually speaking those words to me; we need to remember that God is not going to come down from heaven or appear physically to us, but that he will most likely speak to us through the scriptures or through people.

I went for the interview, and it went really well. I got the job, which paid nearly twice the contract rate that I was earning at that time.

There are also other things we should consider when trying to get our spirits saturated with the word and thoughts of God.

1. *Books / Tapes/ Podcasts*

   It is important that when we are trying to get our job God's way, we surround ourselves with people, books, tapes, music or anything that God can use to speak to us.

2. *Create an atmosphere to hear from God*

   It is imperative that we consciously create an atmosphere and an environment where we can hear God. All truth is parallel; if you have a friend who wants to say something very important to you or if you want to hear something important, you don't go to a busy and noisy place where there are lots of distractions. Instead, you tend to move away from the noise around you and go somewhere quiet where you can hear them without any distractions.

Likewise, when we want to hear from God, we need to create the right atmosphere. Find somewhere quiet where you can read your Bible. It could be in your car or even in the bathroom. Also, go to places where you would generally hear the word of God preached. An environment like the Church, where God's word is being preached is a good place to start. Playing Christian music and listening to audio messages or Christian podcasts are also good options. If on the other hand, you spend the better part of your day socialising with friends, watching movies and partying, it would be more difficult for you to hear from God.

Cultivating a job hunting environment

Psalm 1:1-6 talks about the man who succeeds in all that he does.

> *¹Blessed is the one who does not walk in the step with the wicked or stand in the way that sinners take or sit in the company of mockers,*
> *²But whose delight is in the law of the Lord,*
> *And who meditates on his law day and night.*
> *³That person is like a tree planted by streams of water, which yields its fruit in season*
> *And whose leaf does not wither – whatever they do prospers.*

Psalm 1:1-3 (NIV)

If we want to succeed in our job hunt, we need to learn from the man described above.

This man makes a choice to not walk in the counsel of the ungodly nor sit at the seat of the scornful nor stand in the way of sinners, but delights in God's laws and meditates on them day and night. This man makes a choice to deliberately ignore the counsel given to him by the ungodly. He does not only ignore the counsel of the ungodly, but also meditates on God's word day and night.

The outcome of this man's choice is predictable. The Bible likens him to a tree planted by the rivers of waters. This tree would be evergreen because it gets its supply of water from the surrounding rivers as compared to a tree in the desert. It would always yield fruit in any season because it has what it takes to make it fruitful. Also, its leaf shall not wither.

This is the type of man that we should be aiming to be; a man who refuses to walk in the counsel of the ungodly. God's counsel is different from the counsel of the ungodly. The ungodly will counsel you to tell lies on your resume or C.V. They would counsel you to get a bogus person to give you a good reference or to put your friend's name down as your previous boss. The Bible, however, says that the man who refuses to walk in the counsel of the ungodly and delights in meditating on God's word and acts on it is the one that is blessed. That same man also refuses to stand in the way of sinners. If you stand in the way of sinners, you are likely to pick up their ways. Also, why sit at the seat of the scornful, mocking at those that are doing the right thing and calling them idiots? The Bible also states that the outcome of the ungodly is predictable; it says their ways lead to destruction (*Psalm 1:6*).

We need to make up our minds to do things God's way. The word is the only tool that we need to use to get our jobs, and we need to create the right environment to hear from God and get the word that we will need to stand on against joblessness and failure.

Here are a few bible verses that you could also use as a starting point but remember, look for scriptures that specifically describe the situation you are facing.

> *23For verily I say unto you, That whosoever shall say unto this mountain, Be thou removed, and be thou cast into the sea; and shall not doubt in his heart, but shall believe that those things which he saith shall come to pass; he shall have whatsoever he saith.*
> *24Therefore I say unto you, What things soever ye desire, when ye pray, believe that ye receive them, and ye shall have them.*
>
> Mark 11:23–24
>
> *1The LORD is my shepherd; I shall not want.*
>
> Psalm 23:1
>
> *14And this is the confidence that we have in him, that, if we ask anything according to his will, he heareth us:*

¹⁵And if we know that he hear us, whatsoever we ask, we know that we have the petitions that we desired of him.

1 John 5:14, 15

¹⁹But my God shall supply all your need according to his riches in glory by Christ Jesus.

Philippians 4:19

CHAPTER 5

THE WORD OF GOD AS AN ANCHOR

*U*nderstanding the meaning of words always helps to drive points home. Let me remind you of what the word "anchor" means so we can have a better understanding of the role the word of God should play when applying it to our lives. Dictionary.com defines an anchor as *"a device used for holding fast or checking motion. It is a device used for securing a suspension or cantilever bridge at either end."*

The word of God should be an anchor to our souls. In a world full of distractions and opinions, the word of God should keep us stable because we are assured that the word of God does not change position.

> [12]*That ye be not slothful, but followers of them who through faith and patience inherit the promises.*
> [13]*For when God made promise to Abraham, because he could swear by no greater, he sware by himself,*
> [14]*Saying, Surely blessing I will bless thee, and multiplying I will multiply thee.*
> [15]*And so, after he had patiently endured, he obtained the promise.*
> [16]*For men verily swear by the greater: and an oath for confirmation is to them an end of all strife.*
> [17]*Wherein God, willing more abundantly to shew unto*

> the heirs of promise the immutability of his counsel, confirmed it by an oath:
> [18]That by two immutable things, in which it was impossible for God to lie, we might have a strong consolation, who have fled for refuge to lay hold upon the hope set before us:
> [19]Which hope we have as an anchor of the soul, both sure and stedfast, and which entereth into that within the veil;
> [20]Whither the forerunner is for us entered, even Jesus, made an high priest for ever after the order of Melchisedec.
>
> Hebrews 6:12–20

We do not want to be tossed to and fro by every opinion, so we need God's word as an anchor to keep us steady. When the word of God is received, it is received into our hearts or minds. When negative thoughts come, they come into our minds. We need something to sift the right from the wrong and keep our minds from shifting. The word of God is what would do that sifting. It should be our anchor preventing us from changing our minds when things contrary to what we believe begin to happen.

Similarly, we need to have it settled in our minds that God cannot lie (*Hebrews 6:18*) and that his word is true. The Bible says that it is impossible for God to lie. Impossible means that if you want to do something, you cannot do it because you do not have what it takes to do it. Even if God wanted to lie (but he would never), he cannot because he is God. It is impossible for God to lie. If something is black and God calls it white, it will automatically become white. When he speaks, his word is bound to happen because he is God.

We need to be totally convinced that the word we are holding onto can never fail because it was spoken by a God who cannot lie. Besides, the Bible says that there is no variableness or shadow of turning in God. So God is still saying today what he said yesterday, and he will still be saying it tomorrow. We can, therefore, put our trust and lay our foundation on God's word knowing that it can never change. Granted, we do not know when our job will manifest, but we can be rest assured that it will happen as long as we hold on to the word of God and do not give it up by using it as an anchor to our souls.

Using the word as an anchor would make us walk by faith and not by sight. We will not be governed by what we see, feel, hear, smell or taste. Instead, we will be governed by what the word says.

You have faith in God based on a word that is written in the Bible. It is mandatory that you have a scripture verse from the Bible that you are standing on or depending on regarding your job. You must at least know the chapter and verse or memorise it. That is what you will base your faith on and use as a weapon against negative thoughts. For example, if a negative thought occurs to you that you are going to be unemployed forever, you can say to yourself that, the Bible says in *Philippians 4: 19* that *"My God shall supply all my needs according to His riches in glory by Christ Jesus."*

When things which are contrary to what you have read in your Bible begin to speak to you, you need to say what the Bible says to negate such thoughts. Don't just keep quiet or allow the unhealthy thoughts to linger in your mind. Say something to negate the power of such thoughts. Thoughts that are not allowed to fester, die unborn.

It is the word of God that will keep you sane till what you believe for actually manifests. That is why we need to take our time to meditate on the word before we actually pray.

The word will not work if it is just in our head. Knowledge of the word or its mental acknowledgement will not get us our jobs. It is the word that sinks deep into our spirit and comes out of a convinced or transformed heart that actually produces results.

Everybody has been programmed to believe certain things based on the world's view. The system of the world does not believe God's word. As long as you are in this world, the default way to handle anything is based on the world's view. We, therefore, need to uninstall all those bad programs and reprogram our minds with the word of God.

We need to renew our minds. Renewing our minds with the word of God is what will stand as our anchor when we encounter contrary things.

> [1] I beseech you therefore, brethren, by the mercies of God, that ye present your bodies a living sacrifice, holy, acceptable unto God, which is your reasonable service. [2] And be not conformed to this world: but be ye transformed by the renewing of your mind, that ye may prove what is that good, and acceptable, and perfect, will of God.

> Romans 12:1,2

Paul, the apostle, urges us in the above scripture to transform our minds with the word of God instead of conforming to the world's ways and ideas.

There is a good account that illustrates this in the Bible.

> [1] Then was Jesus led up of the Spirit into the wilderness to be tempted of the devil.
> [2] And when he had fasted forty days and forty nights, he was afterward an hungred.
> [3] And when the tempter came to him, he said, If thou be the Son of God, command that these stones be made bread.
> [4] But he answered and said, It is written, Man shall not live by bread alone, but by every word that proceedeth out of the mouth of God.
> [5] Then the devil taketh him up into the holy city, and setteth him on a pinnacle of the temple,
> [6] And saith unto him, If thou be the Son of God, cast thyself down: for it is written, He shall give his angels charge concerning thee: and in their hands they shall

> bear thee up, lest at any time thou dash thy foot against
> a stone.
> [7]*Jesus said unto him, It is written again, Thou shalt not
> tempt the Lord thy God.*
> [8]*Again, the devil taketh him up into an exceeding high
> mountain, and sheweth him all the kingdoms of the
> world, and the glory of them;*
> [9]*And saith unto him, All these things will I give thee, if
> thou wilt fall down and worship me.*
> [10]*Then saith Jesus unto him, Get thee hence, Satan: for
> it is written, Thou shalt worship the Lord thy God, and
> him only shalt thou serve.*

Matthew 4:1–10

Some people have said that the devil did not physically appear to Jesus, but rather the temptations came as thoughts. Jesus had just finished a forty day fast and was of course hungry. The devil then tempted him to turn stones to bread because he knew Jesus had the power to do it. He also tempted Jesus to cast himself down and worship him. In all three temptations, Jesus replied the devil with the word of God. Jesus in verses 4, 6, and 7 stated to the devil that "*it is written.*" That makes us understand that Jesus used the word as his weapon against the devil's lies. This is the same method in which we need to attack any thought contrary to the word of God. We should never entertain or try to rationalise those thoughts but quickly replace them with what the word of God says.

We need to realise that when we embark on the journey of faith, we will definitely be tempted.

Obviously, the devil will not physically appear to us. But he can use people, articles, music, news or any other form of information to infuse thoughts that are contrary to what we believe. When such negative information comes to us, we need to reply with the word of God. We don't necessarily only reply to people; we can also reply to inanimate things. We reply to them by saying what the word of God says. This might seem illogical, but Mark 10 describes an occasion when Jesus went happily to a fig tree to get some fruit. There was no fruit on the fig tree. The Bible says, "*Jesus replied to the fig tree*". How can you reply to something that does not speak to you? The fig tree must have communicated to Jesus for him to reply to it. If Jesus replied to an inanimate object, we too need to take a leaf out of his book and speak to inanimate objects when they seemingly speak to us.

Since Jesus did not keep quiet when the fig tree had no fruit on it, we too should not keep quiet when we hear any negative information that can instil fear into us while believing in God for a job. For example, if we hear on the news that a hundred employees were laid off or that the unemployment rate is getting higher, we need to declare that our cases are different and, that according to the word of God, we already have our job.

We need to remember that negative thoughts come to challenge the word that we have sown into our hearts. We need to get ourselves to the place where we believe the word of God over and above what these negative words and thoughts are saying to us.

When we keep speaking the word of God to neutralise these opposing and negative thoughts, they will eventually flee (*2 Corinthians 10:5*). However, if we entertain these thoughts, they will punch a hole in what we are building with our faith and it'll just be a matter of time before it eventually collapses.

A little hole can sink a big boat if it stays unchecked. Just as you would waste no time in blocking a hole in your boat, you should waste no time in dispelling negative thoughts before they pollute your mind.

The word of God is the foundation of our faith. Our faith has to be based on something. As a Christian, our faith for our job is based on the word of God. That word is what we build our faith on.

What exactly is a foundation, and how important is a foundation? Dictionary.com says that a foundation is the basis or groundwork of anything. It is the natural or prepared ground or base on which some structure rests. A foundation is designed to have adequate load capacity depending on what needs supporting.

The foundation of your faith should, therefore,

be the word of God. Just as you need to dig deep to lay the foundation of a skyscraper, you also need to dig deep into the word of God to lay the foundation of your faith in his promises. You need to bear in mind that the deeper and stronger your foundation in the word of God is, the easier it will be for it to support your faith. A strong foundation in the word of God would support and withstand any thought that is contrary to what you believe and would also stand the test of time. A shaky foundation, on the other hand, will neither be able to endure the negatives that will be thrown at you nor stand the test of time. You need to spend a considerable amount of time in the word of God.

A story in the Bible that portrays this fact can be found in *Matthew 7:24–27*:

> *[24]Therefore whosoever heareth these sayings of mine, and doeth them, I will liken him unto a wise man, which built his house upon a rock:*
> *[25]And the rain descended, and the floods came, and the winds blew, and beat upon that house; and it fell not: for it was founded upon a rock.*
> *[26]And every one that heareth these sayings of mine, and doeth them not, shall be likened unto a foolish man, which built his house upon the sand:*
> *[27]And the rain descended, and the floods came, and the winds blew, and beat upon that house; and it fell: and great was the fall of it.*
>
> Matthew 7:24–27

This passage refers to a person who acts on the

word and one who does not. Both people were faced with the same situation, but both had varying outcomes depending on whether they acted on the word or not. The one who acted on the word was called wise, while the one who did not act on the word was termed foolish.

Both buildings were subjected to rain, flood, and wind. These elements were big and strong enough to make either building collapse. But whilst one of the buildings stood firm, the other was destroyed. The only difference was in the foundation that held the buildings.

One's foundation on the word of God must, therefore, be strong enough to withstand the type of contrary situation that would make one doubt God's word. You cannot build this type of foundation by hearing the word spoken just once or by overhearing someone quote a scripture. A strong foundation comes by making a conscious effort to put the word in your heart.

It is inevitable that when you start your journey of faith; the rain will descend, the floods will come, and the wind will blow upon what you are building. But you must be prepared; by making sure, that your foundation is strong enough to withstand whatever challenges it. The word of God has to be strongly rooted in your heart, so much so, that it will be able to withstand the attack of the enemy and not cave in when it is attacked or challenged. Take your time to meditate on the word. Spending time building your faith is as important as preparing your foundation before you build. When embarking on a building, we don't just think about the cost of the building above the ground, but we also take account of the building beneath the ground. The building beneath the ground is more important, as it is needed to support the one above the ground.

In summary, laying our foundation is very important and crucial, as it is needed to support what it is about to carry.

CHAPTER 6

EVERY JOB IN THE CITY IS GOD'S

*D*o you know that every job in the city belongs to God? On one occasion when I was believing God for a job, I read *Psalm 50:10–13* and the Lord ministered the scripture to me in a different way.

> *¹⁰For every beast of the forest is mine, and the cattle upon a thousand hills.*
>
> *Psalm 50:10*

God ministered to me that every job in the city belongs to him. Every high, great, and mighty job in the city is his. No matter where the job is, it belongs to God.

> *¹¹I know all the fowls of the mountains: and the wild beasts of the field are mine.*
>
> *Psalm 50:11*

God knows every CEO, Director, Manager, Recruitment Manager, Human Resources Manager, and anyone who has anything to do with the recruitment of the job you are interested in. Also, he knows them by name; he knows where they live and what makes them tick.

He is the omnipotent God, the all-powerful God. He is the omnipresent God; he is everywhere at the same time. He is also the omniscient God, the God who has unlimited knowledge of everything.

Who better to place your trust in than the one who is everywhere at the same time? He is the one who knows what the interviewers are planning to test you on. The God who was in the past, is in the present and knows the future. Not only does he have unlimited knowledge, he is also the most powerful, which means that no one can stop him if he decides to help you. He is the God who opens the door that no man can shut. God has more connections than LinkedIn; he is connected to anybody who is somebody in the natural. He knows everybody.

Some people run around trying desperately to find network connections whilst saying to themselves, "If only I could get someone to connect me to this person or to that person, my job-hunting story would be history."

You don't need anyone to link you to any Manager, CEO, Director or any other person. You don't have to devise a means of hooking up with that person or begging someone to link you up to some top shot. You don't have to stoop so low as to suck up to people just because you want to meet someone who you think can help you. The only connection you need is the connection to God. Why look around when you can look to the only one who has the whole world in his hands? God's LinkedIn page is full of the names of anybody that is somebody. He is connected to everyone who can change your story. Not only is he connected to them, but he can also make them do whatever he wants just like a puppet master pulling the strings of his puppets.

The person who you look up to also has someone they look up to. What if that person you are looking up to genuinely wants to help you, but they cannot help due to some circumstances beyond their control? Stop looking to people for help and start looking to God.

> [2]*Looking unto Jesus the author and finisher of our faith;*
>
> *Hebrews 12:2*

Sometimes, we forget who the God we serve is. We look at problems and forget to look to the one who has the whole world in his hands. We rush around looking for answers everywhere while forgetting that God is near and wants to help.

The Bible tells us in *2 Chronicles 16:9* that the eyes of the Lord run to and fro throughout the whole earth, to show himself strong in the behalf of them whose heart is perfect towards him.

One can interpret this scripture to mean that God's eyes scan the whole earth every day to look through people's hearts trying to find those who are looking up to him. He does not scan the earth looking for people who are looking for jobs, but he scans the whole earth for people who are trusting in him and looking up to him for help.

Proverbs 21:1 also says the following on the subject:

> The king's heart is in the hand of the LORD, as the rivers of water: he turneth it whithersoever he will.
>
> *Proverbs 21:1*

The heart of that HR Manager is in God's hand, and he changes their heart however he wants. We must not try to use our own cunning ways to twist someone's hand to give us a job, manipulate or bribe someone to help us get up the career ladder. We need to look to God in faith, and as we move God by our faith, God will move men to help us.

God does not like it when we look to people for help instead of looking to him. This is spelt out clearly in the scriptures.

Look at *Isaiah 31:1–3.*

> ¹Woe to them that go down to Egypt for help; and stay on horses, and trust in chariots, because they are many; and in horsemen, because they are very strong; but they look not unto the Holy One of Israel, neither seek the LORD!
> ²Yet he also is wise, and will bring evil, and will not call back his words: but will arise against the house of the evildoers, and against the help of them that work iniquity.
> ³Now the Egyptians are men, and not God; and their horses flesh, and not spirit. When the LORD shall stretch out his hand, both he that helpeth shall fall, and he that is holpen shall fall down, and they all shall fail together.

Isaiah 31:1–3

Egypt could be referred to as a type of the world. The above scripture is not saying that if you physically go to Egypt, woe would betide you. Rather, it says that woe betides the person who seeks help from man instead of seeking help from God. We do know that God uses man to help us, but let God decide the method and person whom he has chosen to help us. Let us not solicit or lobby for man's help. God can give us favour in the sight of any man. Let us put our ultimate trust in God and not man.

The Bible has recorded instances of God being displeased with people who had put their trust in man instead of him. One such example was that of King Asa.

> [12]*And Asa in the thirty and ninth year of his reign was diseased in his feet, until his disease was exceeding great: yet in his disease he sought not to the LORD, but to the physicians.*

2 Chronicles 16:12

One should note that God is not against physicians, but that he is against people who seek help from others without acknowledging him. The above quotation from the scripture mentions that Asa did not seek the Lord but instead sought the physicians. The Bible does not record that the physicians were able to help Asa, but it does record that he died.

The Bible also records, in *2 Chronicles 16:7*, that

King Asa of Judah was reprimanded by God because he had relied on the King of Syria instead of relying on God.

When Asa, the King of Judah, faced the Ethiopians and the Lubims – a huge army which had many chariots and horses – he depended on God and won. When he faced a smaller army, he decided to leave God out of the picture and seek help from the King of Syria instead. God sent Hanani, the seer, to tell him that because he had relied on the King of Syria instead of God, he was going to lose the battle.

The Bible makes us understand that the arm of flesh will fail. Man cannot successfully help us if God does not permit him to. If we want help getting a job, it can only be received by seeking God and not man. Man is limited, but with God, all things are possible. Remember, all the jobs in the city belong to God.

CHAPTER 7

THE BATTLE FOR YOUR JOB

*T*he battle to win or lose in every venture takes place in our mind. The dilemma of choosing between going after a job and staying unemployed too happens in our minds, and since this battle takes place in our minds, it must also be won in our minds. The manifestation of your job in the natural is a reflection of the victory that has already been won in your mind.

The battle going on is not one that we can see with our physical eyes. The fact that we cannot actually see ourselves wrestling for our jobs does not mean that we are not actually striving for it .

You might say "I am only looking for a job, I am not in a battle." The Bible tells us that whether we believe it or not, we are in a battle.

> *¹²For we wrestle not against flesh and blood, but against principalities, against powers, against the rulers of the darkness of this world, against spiritual wickedness in high places.*
> *¹³Wherefore take unto you the whole armour of God that ye may be able to withstand in the evil day, and having done all, to stand*

> *Ephesians 6:12-13*

The above scripture implies that we are in a battle and that battle is not one that we engage in with mortals that have flesh and blood, but it is one that we engage in with spiritual beings that we cannot see with our natural eyes. These wicked spirits are in places higher than the earth, and they would do anything to prevent us from getting what we want. Since we are engaged in a spiritual battle, it is inappropriate for us to use man-made weapons to fight in a battle that is not natural. After all, we cannot see these spirits that are trying to hinder us from getting our jobs so why should we use man-made or carnal weapons to fight such battles. We need to use God's armour such as his word in the Bible, prayer, praise and worship to wage such a war.

Another scripture that sheds more light on the fact that there are beings in heavenly places is *Colossians 1:15-17.*

> *Christ is the visible image of the invisible God. For through him, God created everything in the heavenly realms and on earth. He made the things we can see and the things we can't see – such as thrones, kingdoms, rulers, and authorities in the unseen world. Everything was created through him and for him. He existed before anything else, and he holds all creation together.*

Colossians 1:15-17 (NLT)

The above verses highlight some very important points which affect our lives but can be easily overlooked.

- *There is an invisible God.*

- *He created everything.*
- *Christ is the visible image of God.*
- *There are heavenly realms as well as there is the earthly realm which we all know and live in.*
- *There are things we can see, and there are things we cannot see with our physical eyes.*
- *There are thrones, rulers, and authorities in the realm that we cannot see as well as on earth.*
- *These rulers that we cannot see govern and control things. What exactly are they controlling? Who are they governing? What effect do they have on you and I?*

Not to go into too much details, there is a spiritual realm, and there is a natural realm. The spiritual realm is more real than the natural realm, but because we cannot see the supernatural realm as easily as we can see the natural realm, we tend to believe that it does not exist. Things that we cannot see, feel, touch, smell or hear are concluded as being non-existent hence we do not want to accept that there are beings that control what we have in the natural realm. God can have a hand in helping us get our jobs likewise the devil can have a hand in preventing us from getting our jobs; hence the word battle and warring for our jobs. We need to understand that the devil is the author of negative thoughts and anything that disillusions. God on the other hands injects positive thoughts of peace and hope to us.

When you are believing God for a job, it is

more likely that your mind will be flooded with more negative thoughts than positive. Negative thoughts such as *"You are going to be jobless for a while"*, *"How are you going to get a job?"*, *"Look at the countless number of people who do not have jobs"*, *"There are many people more qualified than you out there without jobs"*, *"How are you going to stand out?"*, *"5000 people have applied for the same job"*, *"There are no jobs"*, *"Employers are laying people off"*, *"You are in the wrong field"*, *"You don't have enough experience"*, *"Nobody employs people with those skills"*, *"Your skills are obsolete"*, *"Younger people can do the job better "*, *"You lack interpersonal skills"*. The list could go on and on.

When these thoughts come to you, you need to recognise that you are in a battle. There is a war going on in your mind, and the outcome of this battle will be determined by how you play this game of the mind.

You read a job advert. It describes the type of person they want to hire. They are describing a super human being. You know you do not have what it takes. You are intimidated by the advert.

What do you do when your mind is being bombarded with negative thoughts? What do you do when everything around you agrees with the negative thoughts flooding your mind? What do you do when there is no light at the end of the tunnel? What do you do when you see yourself as a grasshopper in the face of the giant called joblessness?

I want to share the story of a young boy who faced a challenge that was too big for him.

The name of this boy was David, the youngest of twelve sons of Jesse. There was a war between the Israelites and the Philistines during the reign of King Saul. David was too young to be enlisted in the army, but three of his brothers were of age and were in the army. He was sent by his father to give some food to his brothers. It was while he was at the battlefield that he overheard a 9 feet giant called Goliath challenging any member of King Saul's army to a fight. Though David was no match for Goliath, he decided to take him on. To everyone's utter amazement, David won the battle. There were some principles that David applied which could also be applied by you when you are looking for a job and it seems you don't have what it takes.

> As he was talking with them, Goliath, the Philistine champion from Gath, stepped out from his lines and shouted his usual defiance, and David heard it. Whenever the Israelites saw the man, they all fled from him in great fear.
>
> 1 Samuel 17:23-24

Fear not

David heard Goliath's defiance against Israel, and so did the Israelite army. While Israel fled in great fear, David stood. What made David stand? What made Israel flee? Neither David nor the Israelites had physically engaged Goliath in battle at that point, but the Israelites had already lost that battle in their minds even before it began.

All through the Bible, you would notice that if God wants to help, he first commands us not to fear (*Joshua 8:1; Deuteronomy 31:6; Isaiah 41:10*). Fear cripples and paralyses us. Once you are paralysed by fear, you will not be victorious. Fear will prevent you from acting in faith. Faith and fear cannot both be in the same boat. It would have to be one or the other. If you let fear in, faith will go out of the window. But if you let faith in, fear will diminish.

Refuse to be intimidated

David heard the same words that everyone else heard, but his reaction was different. He was not intimidated. Did David have every right to be intimidated? Yes, he did. He was not in the army. He did not have the prerequisites needed to serve in the army. He was not even qualified to apply. Remember that he was only sent to deliver food to his brothers. He was of the wrong age. He had the wrong height. He had the wrong build. In a nutshell, he was not the type of person they were looking for.

Despite all these shortcomings, David refused to be intimidated by Goliath. Goliath was nine feet and nine inches tall. He was a giant compared to David. Not only was he tall, but he also had a helmet of brass on his head, was armed with a coat of mail made with five thousand shekels of brass. Additionally, he had greaves of brass upon his legs, a target of brass between his shoulders, and a spear like a weaver's beam which weighed six hundred shekels of iron. His credentials were enough to intimidate even the best of the best. Yet, David refused to be intimidated.

By the way, those who could stand up against Goliath were too intimidated to step out. Goliath kept raging, ranting, calling out to someone to heed his challenge. The Israelites looked at Goliath and at themselves, and they concluded that Goliath was going to kill them. They concluded that they were no match for Goliath even before they physically tackled him. They did this because they lost the battle in their minds before it even began.

David, on the other hand, also heard Goliath. He looked at Goliath, and instead of comparing the giant to himself, I believe that David compared the giant to God because David knew that God was on his side and that God was going to help him fight the battle. I believe he said to himself, "This is a situation for God to get the glory. Truly, I am no match for this guy but my God is well able". He knew he could not fight Goliath in his own his strength and that the battle belonged to God and not to him. The actual battle was going on in David's mind, and I believe he was saying to himself, "Surely, I can do this with God on my side. Indeed, I am destined to win".

You too need to reject any feelings of intimidation.

Intimidation robs you of your confidence and makes you feel insecure and inferior. Feelings of inferiority will reflect in how you carry yourself and can be seen in your body language by potential employers. If you are intimidated, your body language will portray messages that say, "I am not good enough. There is someone else better than me".

Fair enough, it is easy to feel intimidated when we see other candidates who we think have more experience and skills or are more eloquent than we are. But we should remember that the God factor in our lives is bigger than what we lack. Instead of comparing ourselves to these superior competitors, let us compare their strength with the might of our God. When we do that, we will see that they are no match for God.

Know who you are in Christ

David knew he was circumcised and Goliath was an uncircumcised Philistine. He knew that he had a covenant with God. Knowing that God was on his side made him confident that he was going to defeat Goliath. That is why he wanted to know what he would get if he killed Goliath. If he did not think he could kill Goliath, he would not have asked for what he would get. He knew that God was able to help him against Goliath, so he asked, "What is in it for me?" You need to know who you are in Christ when negative thoughts and feelings of insecurity threaten you.

Ignore people who say you cannot do it
Eliab, David's brother, tried to remind David that he was no match for Goliath. He reminded David that he only had the experience of looking after a few sheep. Note that Eliab used the descriptive word "few" to emphasise that he did not have what was needed to defeat Goliath. David ignored him and asked someone else about what reward was to be given to the person that killed Goliath.

In your search for the job of your dreams, you will come across people who would be more than happy to tell you about their own failures and that there is no need for you to try. They will tell you that they are trying to prevent you from being disappointed and disillusioned. You need to ignore such people and turn to other people who will encourage you to go for your dream job.

What do they know anyway? If God is for you, no one can be against you.

Recount past victories
When Saul said to David that he was just a youth and could not go against Goliath. David recounted his past victories. He told Saul about how he smote the lion and bear that came after his father's sheep. Recounting past victories is a great weapon against the enemy because it silences the voice of doubt and unbelief.

Remind yourself of the times God helped you

win battles. If God did it then, he would do it again.

Declare what you believe
David believed that he was going to smite Goliath as he had smitten the bear and lion that came for his father's sheep. He was not timid to declare it. He declared that Goliath was going to be history, and that is what happened.

Never recount your fears or past failures, instead recount and declare your victory. The fear, defeat and intimidation will be dispelled when you keep declaring your victory.

Personal testimony
This reminds me of a time in my life when I was invited for an interview for a job with one of the main consultancy firms in London, England in 1997. The interview was going to last the whole day, and at the end of the day, I was going to be told the outcome. The process was going to start with a technical written test and then an interview with a panel of three people. Lastly, there was going to be a practical assessment to see if I would be able to fit into the team.

However, I did not know all this at that time apart from the fact that I had been shortlisted for the interview and the outcome was going to be decided on the day. The agent who put me forward for the job instructed me to see him before attending the interview so that he would be able to prepare me for it.

It is important to note that, in those days, agents were very discreet about giving you the details of employers so other agents would not poach their jobs.

For some reason, I misconstrued his instructions and thought the interview was going to be at the agent's office.

The day before the interview, I realised that I did not have enough time to prepare. Negative thoughts kept coming to me about how I did not have what it took to get the job. Also, I had a lot of technical things to go over before the interview, and I knew that it was impossible for me to go over all the things I planned to revise. I had two options, either to spend the whole night revising or to depend on God. I would have loved to spend the whole night preparing, but there was no guarantee that I would be tested on what I planned on preparing as the topic was too wide and I could be tested on anything. I also recollected a time when I read the whole Informix 4gl technical manual before an interview and didn't get the job. I made up mind that I was going to do it God's way and meditate on his word.

I meditated on the story of the woman who did not have enough oil. Elisha the prophet said she should borrow vessels. The story is from *2 Kings*

4:1–7, and in my Bible study notes from 1997, I wrote the following:

She was a widow; she had to live with the fact that her husband was dead and that she had to raise her two sons alone.

The creditor came for his money, and she had none. There was nothing valuable for the creditor to take or for him to sell. He, therefore, decided to take her two sons as slaves. This was a nightmare for this widow. It was a critical situation. A normal mother would trade all she has to protect her children. She had lost her husband, and now, she was about to lose her children for not being able to pay off her husband's debt.

She dashed off to Elisha for help. Elisha listened to her and said, "*What do you have in your house?*" At first, she thought, "I don't have anything. I mean, they are coming to take my priciest possession, and you are asking me what I have. If I had anything, wouldn't I have traded them for the lives of my only sons? Do you think I would be standing here asking for your help? I don't have anything". Then, she thought again, "Hang on a minute. I have a pot of oil". She was a bit hesitant to mention it, but she did. She did not know if the pot of oil was relevant to the situation or not. She forgot that the Bible says there is no restraint on the Lord to save by many or by few (*1 Samuel 14:6*).

Elisha's face lit up, and he said, "*Go, borrow thee*

vessels abroad of thy neighbours, even empty vessels, borrow not a few. And when thou art come in, thou shalt shut the door upon thee and upon thy sons, and shalt pour out into all those vessels, and thou shalt set aside that which is full."

She could have said, "This is a life and death situation. I am serious here, man of God. Can't you see that this is just a pot of oil?" She could have also said, "It is our borrowing that got us into this trouble, and you are saying I should borrow again." She could have refused to do what Elisha said because it sounded stupid (Go borrow vessels from all your neighbours and keep pouring into empty pots and then sell the oil to pay off your debt). How can one pot of oil fill many pots of oil? That was not logical. She could have reasoned it out, and out of courtesy, said, "Thanks" but then ignored what he said she should do. She could have given a million and one reasons why Elisha's advice could never work or ever amount to anything, but she made a choice to obey the man of God even though it sounded foolish. She made up her mind to act on what he said, though her mind was screaming that it made no sense.

The solution to our problems is in the word of God. It is up to us to take the word, believe it, and act on it. She had to have walked by faith and not by sight. A woman her age should have known that one pot of oil could not fill many vessels. The quantity needed to fill the vessels was greater than the quantity of oil contained in one pot. She did not need anyone to tell her that. It was a no-brainer. In other words, it was very obvious.

If she had rationalised that it would take more than one jar of oil to fill the many empty jars she borrowed, she would not have acted on the word. She had to have looked into the spirit realm and at the bigness of her God. She then said to herself, "Nothing is impossible with God. It seems impossible in the natural, but with God, it is possible. I trust God. I do not know how he is going to do it, but he is God. I cannot fathom how he would fix this issue, but I am not God. I need to believe and leave the acting and fixing of this issue to him".

She refused to reason and threw all logical reasoning out. She went ahead to do what Elisha said. This woman had to go home. Her mind must have been shouting, "You are an idiot. One jar of oil to fill many jars of oil – fool, they are definitely going to take your sons away". She had to ignore those words and go from one neighbour to another borrowing vessels. She had every opportunity to waver on the way. She had every opportunity to turn back. She had every reason to back down, but she did not. She went ahead convinced of nothing else but the word, and the barrel of oil did not fail. Because she acted on Elisha's command, she paid off her debt.

From what I read, I made up my mind to believe the word of God that said, "*What things soever you desire, when you pray, believe that you receive them, and you shall have them."* It sounded foolish and illogical to me because I knew that other candidates were probably spending their time reading manuals and all, but I decided to take God at his word. God knew that I did not have enough time to cover all the topics in the manual, but he still said that if I prayed, I should just believe. I decided to act on God's word.

I armed myself with the teachings of *Mark 11:23-24* and *1 John 5:14-15*

> *For verily I say unto you, That whosoever shall say unto this mountain, Be thou removed, and be thou cast into the sea; and shall not doubt in his heart, but shall believe that those things which he saith shall come to pass; he shall have whatsoever he saith.*
> *Therefore I say unto you, What things soever ye desire, when ye pray, believe that ye receive them, and ye shall have them.*

> *Mark 11:23-24*

> *And this is the confidence that we have in him, that, if we ask any thing according to his will, he heareth us: And if we know that he hear us, whatsoever we ask, we know that we have the petitions that we desired of him.*
> *With these scriptures, I asked God for the job and believed that I had received the job even before attending the interview.*

> *1 John 5:14-15*

On the day of the interview, I arrived at the agent's office with barely 10 to 15 minutes left. He told me that I was going to be late for the interview as it was not going to take place at his office. He asked if I had any money for a taxi to the venue of the interview, and I said "No" as I had my travel card and debit card with me. In those days, you paid for your taxi fare by cash and not with your card, and if I decided to go by train, the tube, or a bus, I would have been very late. So the agent called a taxi for me and gave me £10 for my fare. I could have given up at that time and said, "I can't get this job. I am late for the interview. What type of impression am I going to portray?" But like the lady in the story with her two sons, I decided that God's word was true and that the fact that I arrived early or late was irrelevant. I had not deliberately decided to arrive late; I had thought the interview was being held at the agent's office and did not realise it was being held somewhere else. I believed that the job was still mine because God's word said it was mine.

I arrived at the interview late, and they ushered me into an empty room with a desk, a question paper, and a pen to take the technical test. I sat down, looked at the test, and did not understand the question. I still refused to doubt. I kept thanking God that the job was mine. I looked at the question again, and all of a sudden, it became clear to me what they were asking and what I was supposed to do. I answered the questions, and when the time ended, they came in, collected the exam paper, and went out to mark it. They came back to say that I was through to the next stage of the screening process. This was a verbal interview with a panel of three, which went well. Then, they told me that we were going to the pub for a drink. I did not realise that this was also a part of the interview process and that they wanted to use this to assess whether I would fit into the team or not. I went along with them and ordered orange juice, while they all ordered beer.

After this, we went back to the office, and they hinted that I was quiet. I could see that they were not keen on giving me the job because they thought I would not fit in. They went out to deliberate, and I kept thanking God that the job was mine. I refused to be moved by what I saw and held on to the word. They then offered me the job on that day.

I had put the word of God to work, and I refused to be moved by what I saw. I depended on God, and he got me the job despite the fact that my method was illogical and unreasonable.

CHAPTER 8

IT'S TIME TO PRAY

*I*f you already have the word as an anchor and have meditated on it, perhaps you are now ready to pray. But before you pray, there are a few things you need to bear in mind.

1. *You will need to take the scripture at face value*

   The promise of God in Christ are *"yea"* and *"Amen"* (*2 Corinthians 1:20*). If the Bible says that you should believe that you receive when you pray, then after you pray, you must believe even if you do not see, feel, or hear anything positive. You need to set your face like a flint or a stone. When we say that something is set in stone, it means that it is difficult to move and that it is rigid. We should not be tossed to and fro by what we see or hear. We should be fully persuaded that what we believe, will come to pass.

2. *You need to believe you receive NOW*

   You will have to leave the place of prayer, knowing that God has heard and released your job. Not that God is going to answer someday, but that the moment you pray, He will immediately release your job..

3. *Your faith should be active and not passive*

Your faith is the currency that is going to pull your job from the spiritual realm into the natural realm. Your faith has a voice which means there is a way, you speak when you have faith. I don't mean forcing yourself to speak in a certain way but you will speak with a conviction that comes from your heart, that you have what the word of God says you have. The voice of faith says, "I believe, therefore I speak".

Faith also has an action. The action of faith, thanks God for the manifestation even though nothing has happened in the natural realm. For example, a woman that is expecting a child could start buying baby clothes and all the paraphernalia that comes with having a baby. She does not need any one to tell her how to act. Likewise, someone genuinely acting in faith will have a corresponding faith action. You will not need anyone to tell you how to act. Your action would also come from a heart that is convinced that you have received your job from God.

4. *You must look at the answer with your eyes of faith*

What you see is what you get. You need to envision yourself with that job. You need to be able to see yourself waking up in the morning and going out to work. You need to be able to see yourself at that desk and in that business meeting. You cannot see yourself broke and unable to pay your bills if you believe you have got your job. The picture of yourself that you see with the eyes of your spirit is what will indeed come to pass. If you see yourself with your job, no one can stop that job from coming to pass.

5. *You need to make sure you are not living in open sin and rebellion*

The bible says if you regard iniquity in your heart, the Lord will not hear you (Psalm 66:18). Make sure you are not living in known sin and that you are doing all you know to do.

6. *You need to forgive and release people who have offended you*

We need to forgive people their trespasses, if we want God to forgive us and hear our prayers (*Matthew 5:39, 40).*

How do you pray?

You pray by simply presenting God's promise to him. It could be something along the lines of the following statements:

"Father, you said in your word in Mark 11:23 that whatsoever I desire, when I pray I should believe that I receive it and I will have it. Lord I desire a job with

the following… I ask you for it now in Jesus' name. Lord, I thank you that I believe I have the job because I have asked according to your word".

You can then leave that place of prayer believing that you have the job. Nothing may change in the physical realm. You may not feel happy, but that is all right because you have received your job by faith and not by your feelings. You need to start rejoicing because the word says you already have your job. Keep on looking at the word till your job manifests. These are some scriptures that you may want to use to pray for your job.

> *23For verily I say unto you, That whosoever shall say unto this mountain, Be thou removed, and be thou cast into the sea; and shall not doubt in his heart, but shall believe that those things which he saith shall come to pass; he shall have whatsoever he saith.*
> *24Therefore I say unto you, What things soever ye desire, when ye pray, believe that ye receive them, and ye shall have them.*
>
> *Mark 11:23-24*
>
> *23And in that day ye shall ask me nothing. Verily, verily, I say unto you, whatsoever ye shall ask the Father in my name, he will give it you.*
> *24Hitherto have ye asked nothing in my name: ask, and ye shall receive, that your joy may be full.*
>
> *John 16:23-24*
>
> *19But my God shall supply all your need according to his riches in glory by Christ Jesus. Now unto God and our Father be glory for ever and ever. Amen.*
>
> *Philippians 4:19*

PART II

STAND FIRMLY AND HOLD YOUR GROUND

CHAPTER 10

ACT ON THE WORD OF GOD

*F*aith means acting on the word and doing what the word says you should do. You will never receive from God if you do not exercise your faith on what you believe.

> [18]Yea, a man may say, Thou hast faith, and I have works: shew me thy faith without thy works, and I will shew thee my faith by my works.
> [19]Thou believest that there is one God; thou doest well: the devils also believe, and tremble.
> [20]But wilt thou know, O vain man, that faith without works is dead?
>
> *James 2:18-20*

It may interest you to know that although the love of God is unconditional, his promises are conditional. There is a myth that since God knows our needs and we have prayed, he will answer and as a result of this, there is no obligation on our part to work by faith. By doing this, we have shifted all the responsibility to God and are not exercising our faith. There is a God part to the equation, but there is also a human part. Just as in the natural world, 1 + 1 = 2, God plays his part, and we too have our part to play before we can balance the equation. Unfortunately, most people expect God to play his part without playing their own part. God is under no obligation to answer our prayers if we do not act on the word or walk by faith. This has been spelt clearly in *Hebrews 11:6*.

> *⁶But without faith it is impossible to please him: for he that cometh to God must believe that he is, and that he is a rewarder of them that diligently seek him.*
>
> *Hebrews 11:6*

If you have prayed for a job and you are waiting on God to answer it sometime in the future, then you are not walking by faith. Once you have prayed by faith, you will believe that God has already answered your prayers and that you have received your job despite not seeing anything. You will leave the place of prayer knowing that it is a matter of "when the job materialises" and not "if the job materialises." It is inevitable that the job will materialise because God can never lie and his word can never fail.

For instance, if you apply for a mortgage and you receive a pre-approved certificate or a conditional offer, which states the conditions that you need to fulfil before the loan can be released to you. Without you fulfilling the conditions, the mortgage provider is under no obligation to release the mortgage.

Would you then go around saying that you are waiting on the mortgage provider to release the loan? No, you would not because you have not fulfilled your own part. But most people treat

God like that; they pray to him, ask him for a job, but their prayers are not prayers of faith. Yet, they expect God to answer when *Hebrews 11:6* clearly states that without faith, you cannot please him

To receive from God, you have to act on what the word says. You can be rest assured that he will keep his promise once you fulfil your own part of the deal. *Psalm 89:34* assures us that God will not break his promise

Let us assume that I am looking for a job and I find a scripture that I want to stand on. I find *Mark 11:23-24* and want to use it as my basis for praying for a job..

> [23]*For verily I say unto you, That whosoever shall say unto this mountain, Be thou removed, and be thou cast into the sea; and shall not doubt in his heart, but shall believe that those things which he saith shall come to pass; he shall have whatsoever he saith.*
> [24]*Therefore I say unto you, What things soever ye desire, when ye pray, believe that ye receive them, and ye shall have them.*
>
> Mark 11:23-24

These verses provide clear instructions that I could take to make my desires materialise in the physical:

1. *Have a clear desire*
2. *Pray for what I desire*

3. *Believe I received my desire when I prayed*
4. *Not to entertain any thoughts of doubt*
5. *Believe that the things I prayed for shall come to pass*

In the points listed above, I mentioned that I need to believe. Most people confuse hoping with believing. Hoping for something is not believing for that thing and believing for something is not hoping for that thing. They are similar but different enough to make you miss the difference between them if you use both interchangeably. Hoping is saying "I do not have it now but at a future date, I will have it". On the other hand, believing is saying "I have it now" even though there may not be any physical evidence to prove that I have it. Believing goes a step further than merely hoping for something. *Hebrews 11:1* says, "*Faith is the substance of what we hope for.*" Having the substance of what you hope for is faith.

If you have the evidence of something, it is as good as having that thing. The evidence of something proves that it exists. That is the reason why evidence is tenable in court. Once you can prove that you have the evidence, it is generally agreed that the thing, though not seen, exists.

In the same way, our faith in the word of God is the evidence that the thing we are believing for actually exists.

In the case of a job, once you have prayed for it according to the word of God (take, for instance,

Mark 11:23,24), you must believe that the job exists. You must believe that God has released the job. Granted, there may be a time lag between when God releases the job in the spiritual realm and when it actually manifests here on earth, but we have to look through the eye of faith and not the eye of hope. The eye of faith says "I have it now though it has not been revealed to my five senses".

There is a saying that actions speak louder than words. This also holds true in the realm of faith. There is a difference between the action of someone who is walking by faith and that of someone who is just hoping that one day, he or she would get a job. In fact, Jesus was recorded many times saying, "*Your faith has made you whole.*" He was never recorded saying that "Your hope has made you whole." This, therefore, implies that we need faith to be whole or in this case, to get our job. The story of Joshua and the Israelites at the wall of Jericho is that of people who walked by faith in the midst of a hopeless situation.

Joshua 6:1–2 states as follows:

> *¹Now Jericho was straitly shut up because of the children of Israel: none went out, and none came in. ²And the LORD said unto Joshua, See, I have given into thine hand Jericho, and the king thereof, and the mighty men of valour.*
>
> *Joshua 6:1–2*

God said that he had already given Israel the land, but in the natural realm, that was not the case. To the natural eyes, there was no change; the situation was still the same. Did God lie? No, God did not lie and cannot lie *(Titus 1:2)*. The Israelites could not get into Jericho, and those in Jericho could not go out. The fortified wall was a barrier to them. Though Israel was outside Jericho's fortified walls in the natural realm, in the spirit realm, those walls had collapsed. It looked as if the walls were secure in the natural world, but in reality, the walls were down because God said he had given Jericho to Israel. To get the natural to line up with the spiritual, the Israelites had to walk by faith. If they had not walked by faith, though the walls were down in the spiritual realm, the same collapsed walls in the spiritual realm, would never have manifested or materialised in the natural realm.

The picture of Jericho and the Israelites can represent the picture of the job market. The market is saturated. Some people fear losing their jobs, others fear quitting a job that they don't enjoy whilst some are content with getting government handouts. The word of God says, *"As long as you believe when you pray, you already have the job."* It is not saying that you are going to have the job , but that you already have it. It is a done deal.

In the natural realm, unemployment may still be staring you in the face; your debtors may still be chasing you; mockers may still be making fun of you, and you may still be collecting government handouts, but if God says you have your desired job, then you have it. However, it takes faith to bring things that are in the spirit realm into the natural realm.

Fear, doubt, and unbelief stop our faith from manifesting in the natural realm even though it has been certified in the spirit realm. Sometimes, it is good to look at things from God's perspective. God looks at the spirit realm and speaks based on what is in the spirit realm. Everything that we see today in the natural realm first existed in the spirit realm; so, we need to see things the way God sees them.

2 Corinthians 4:18 says as follows:

> *[18]While we look not at the things which are seen, but at the things which are not seen: for the things which are seen are temporal; but the things which are not seen are eternal.*
>
> *2 Corinthians 4:18*

The fact that you cannot see your job in the natural realm is irrelevant. If God says that your job exists, then it exists. Your faith is the currency that will bring the job from the spiritual realm into the physical realm. The things that you see now are transient and will change as long as you act on the word of God by faith.

CHAPTER 11

THE POWER OF FOCUS

*O*nce you have prayed for your job, you need to focus. You need to set your face like a flint and determine that nothing is going to make you lose sight of what you have set out to achieve.

There is a very interesting story in the Bible that demonstrates this. It is the story of when God decided to take Elijah to heaven by a whirlwind.

Elijah was a prophet in Israel during the reign of Kings Ahab, Ahaziah and Joram. Elisha was Elijah's protégée. Elisha was very impressed with his master because God had used him to perform many mighty miracles such as raising a widow's son, calling fire down from heaven to kill the prophets of Baal, causing the rain to cease for three and a half years and much more. Elisha, the protégée of Elijah, got wind of the fact that his master was going to be taken away to heaven (by a whirlwind). Because Elisha was very faithful, his master asked him if he wanted anything before he left. Elisha asked for a double portion of his master's anointing which in essence meant that Elisha wanted to be able to perform double the miracles that his master had performed. His goal was to have twice the impact that Elijah had in his lifetime. Elijah replied that Elisha had asked for a hard thing, but if he saw him leave the earth, his request will be granted. This protégée then made up his mind that he was going to hang around Elijah till he departed. His desire for this gift made him persistently follow Elijah despite the fact that he had to face several situations that could have broken his focus.

Elijah says to Elisha in *2 Kings 2:3*, "*Tarry here, I pray thee; for the Lord hath sent me to Bethel."*

Elisha replies, "*As the Lord liveth, and as thy soul liveth, I will not leave thee."*

Elisha's attitude is one that we need to emulate when we are waiting for the manifestation of the job we have prayed for. We need to make up our minds that come hell or high water, we are going to hold on to the word till our job manifests. We need to decide that we are going to focus on the word and nothing else.

In verse 3, the sons of the prophets that were at Bethel came to Elisha and said, "*Knowest thou that the Lord will take away thy master from thy head today? And he said, Yea, I know it; hold ye your peace"*

The sons of the prophets, though they were telling Elisha the truth, were there as distractors to make him lose his focus. Elisha was smart enough to realise this and told them to hold their peace. In other words, he said, "Mind your own business;

I am fully aware of the fact, and I can handle it. I know my master is going to be taken but I am working on a plan and I would appreciate it if you do not let me lose my focus". If it was an insensitive person, they would have asked those prophets to tell them where, when, and how they had gotten the information. Elisha knew that by hanging around these prophets, he was going to be distracted; so, he made up his mind that he was going to give them short and sharp answers so that they would leave him alone.

Just as Elisha refused to lose his focus because of the prophets, we too should refuse to lose our focus by engaging in unnecessary conversations with distractors. People may unintentionally try to distract us into taking our eyes off the word by saying things such as the following: "Do you know that so and so went to the library and studied, he networked with a lot of people, and he got a brilliant job" or "So and so has a friend that is a recruitment consultant, his friend put in a good word for him and he got a job" or "I know a person that lied on his resume and got a job that he was not qualified to get". You need to be sensitive to know that if you pay attention to these distractors long enough, you will soon take your eyes off the word and focus on things that are not guaranteed to get you your job. Just as Elisha refused to take his eyes off Elijah, we should refuse to take our eyes off the word.

In verse 4, Elijah again said to Elisha, *"Tarry*

here, I pray thee for the Lord has sent me to Jericho." Someone else might have been offended at Elijah's attempt to put Elisha off from following him, but not Elisha. He wanted a double portion of Elijah's anointing and was not going to let offence, anger or irritation make him break his focus. He replied to Elijah again with the same words, *"As the Lord liveth, and as thy soul liveth, I will not leave thee."*

Legitimate things may also be a potential source of distraction for you and may make you want to lose focus, but be determined not to let go of the word.

In verse 5, the sons of the Prophets who were at Jericho too told Elisha that his master was going to be taken away from him. Again, they were there to distract, but Elisha was determined not to give up. His response again was *"Hold ye your peace."*

We must never be tired of saying the correct thing. We must be constant and persistent about what we want. Like a bulldog, we need to hold on to the word and not lose our focus.

You may not have prophets or masters saying anything to you, but the news on the radio or television may be speaking to you. Articles you read in the newspaper may inject thoughts of fear. How about the retrenchment you heard about on the news? How about what your colleagues told you about the saturated job market? How about the negative report you just heard about so and so who lost their job? All these things are speaking to you just like the sons of the prophets were speaking to Elisha. How are you going to respond to them?

How about the fact that you have no money and that you cannot pay your bills and that you owe someone money? How about the fact that your biological clock is ticking, and that you have nowhere to stay?

All these situations are speaking to you just like the prophets were speaking to Elisha. How are you going to respond? Are you going to agree with the distractors or like Elisha, are you going to say "Hold ye your peace"? I pray that you will be able to say to whatever or whoever tries to break your focus, to hold their peace. Keep looking at the word. Do not let it go. Hold fast to that which you already have and watch God make your job a reality.

CHAPTER 12

Do not be distracted

S omeone said, "*Satan can never schedule your destruction, he can only schedule your distraction.*"

The Bible has examples of people who were distracted and ended up missing their destiny. One of such stories is that of Samson.

Samson was born when Israel was under the rule and oppression of the Philistines. He was to help free the Israelites from the Philistines. He was instructed to never cut his hair. He was so strong that he killed a lion with his bare hands and successfully defeated a thousand Philistines. He did so many things that a normal person could not do. However, Samson got distracted by a beautiful lady called Delilah. He was intrigued by her beauty that he did not mind doing anything just to please her. She asked for the secret of his strength. At first, he lied to her but after a few persuasions, he told her that he was not allowed to cut his hair. She informed the Philistines who later captured and imprisoned him. While in prison, his hair started to grow again. One day the Philistines brought him out before a crowd of people that had gathered in a temple to celebrate his capture. Samson prayed to God for strength, leaned on the pillars that supported the temple and killed himself along with all the Philistines who were in the temple.

Samson was distracted by Delilah's beauty (*Judges 13–14*). This distraction was what led to his downfall. Needless to say, he took a lot of Philistines with him when he died. The price he had to pay for his distraction was high. It cost him his life. We should realise that distractions are one of the top instruments that the devil uses to defeat Christians.

In Will Smith's movie "Focus", a con artist and his accomplice distracted people in order to steal from them. That is exactly the same way that the devil tries to con Christians. He distracts them, and then, while they are not looking, he takes their belongings.

When you set out on a mission to get your job, you need to be sensitive to things that could potentially distract you from achieving your goal. Distraction could come in different shapes and forms.

It could come in these forms:

- *Disruption in your family*
- *Quarrels with your spouse, children, etc.*
- *Conflict at work*
- *Conflict with relatives*
- *Problems with things; for example, cars, houses, etc.*

- *Offence*
- *Insult*
- *Evictions*
- *Overload of work*
- *Friend's visiting*
- *Extended family having issues*
- *Illnesses*

This list is not exhaustive. We need to be very vigilant while we are believing God for our job because some of these things that infringe on our peace could actually just be distractions from the devil.

The Bible says the following in *1 Peter 5:8-9*:

> *[8]Be sober, be vigilant; because your adversary the devil, as a roaring lion, walketh about, seeking whom he may devour:*
> *[9]Whom resist stedfast in the faith, knowing that the same afflictions are accomplished in your brethren that are in the world.*

1 Peter 5:8-9

We normally use the term vigilant in situations when we do not want something to creep up on us. A distraction is not something that is confrontational. If someone confronts you about taking what belongs to you, you are aware of what they want to do. But in the case of a distraction, you are not fully aware because the distractor is making you focus on something else, so that he can take what you are not focusing on.

The price you would pay for getting distracted is very costly, so we need to be sober and vigilant.

Another story in the Bible about someone who was distracted can be found in *1 Kings 13*

In this story, God sent a young prophet to Bethel to warn King Jeroboam that the false priests who had been offering fake and unacceptable sacrifices were going to be destroyed. Because the prophecy was one of doom, Jeroboam the King raised his hand to grab the young prophet. In the process, his hand dried up. Jeroboam then pleaded with the young prophet to pray for him. The prophet prayed, and Jeroboam's hand was restored. In a bid to thank the young prophet, Jeroboam invited him home to dine with him. The prophet replied that he had been given specific instructions not to eat, drink or go back the same way he came. He insisted that he was going to abide by the instructions God had given him.

On his way home, he met an older prophet who told him that he had received another instruction from God. He was informed that he could now eat and drink. Instead of the younger prophet to insist that God did not reveal this to him and that he needed to check with God, he got distracted by the fact that this prophet was older and more experienced than him. He did not consider the fact that God never changes what he has said. Anyway, he was distracted from his assignment by this older prophet. He followed the older prophet to his house and dined with him. As soon as he finished eating, the older prophet prophesied that, the younger prophet was going to be killed by a lion because of his disobedience. He was distracted, and then he disobeyed. He was killed on his way home by a lion as predicted by the older prophet.

This story is a classic example of giving in to distraction. The Prophet clearly heard the word of God that he should eat no bread and drink no water. The Prophet who was distracted was not sensitive enough to recognise that he was being distracted, and he paid dearly for his mistake with his life. If the Old Prophet had said, "Do not obey God, Come and dine with me", the younger prophet would have refused. But he was cunningly distracted and lured away.

We should be very sensitive when we are believing God while looking for our job because distractors will come. They will tell us what God has not said, but we need to be sure about what God has said. The Bible is very clear about God having neither variableness nor a shadow of turning. Once we have read God's word in the Bible, we need to hold onto it and not receive any other instruction that contradicts the word of God. We do not need to start running around looking for Prophets to tell us what is already in the Bible. If someone prophesies to you, his words should be tested and the prophecy should also be a confirmation of what God has already told you. The Bible says in *Romans 8:14*, *"As many as are led by the spirit of God, they are the sons of God."*

Another such person in the Bible was David, whose subject of distraction was Bathsheba (*2 Samuel 11:1–4*).

> ¹*And it came to pass, after the year was expired, at the time when kings go forth to battle, that David sent Joab, and his servants with him, and all Israel; and they destroyed the children of Ammon, and besieged Rabbah. But David tarried still at Jerusalem.*
> ²*And it came to pass in an eveningtide, that David arose from off his bed, and walked upon the roof of the king's house: and from the roof he saw a woman washing herself; and the woman was very beautiful to look upon.*
> ³*And David sent and inquired after the woman. And one said, Is not this Bathsheba, the daughter of Eliam, the wife of Uriah the Hittite?*
> ⁴*And David sent messengers, and took her; and she came in unto him, and he lay with her;*
>
> *2 Samuel 11:1–4*

While the Kings were on the battlefield, David stayed at home in Jerusalem. While he was walking on the roof of his house, he got distracted by a beautiful woman washing herself. This distraction cost David the life of his son.

Another example is that of Mary and Martha. Mary and Martha were sisters. When Jesus went to their house to visit, Mary sat at Jesus's feet and was listening to what he taught while Martha was distracted by the dinner she was preparing.

She went to Jesus and asked him to tell Mary off for not helping her with the dinner. But Jesus said *"Martha, you are worried and upset over many things! There is one thing that is worth being concerned about, Mary has discovered it, and it will not be taken from her."*

1 Corinthians 7:35 also tells us to attend upon the Lord without distraction. In our quest for a job God's way, we need to ensure that we stay focused and not get distracted.

Likewise, there are examples of people in the Bible who were not distracted.

Jesus did not get distracted when he was tempted by the devil. Though Jesus was hungry after the 40-day fast, he refused to give in to the temptation and distraction of the devil.

The five wise virgins in the story of the five wise and five foolish virgins also did not get distracted by the begging and pleading of the five foolish ones. Though it is more blessed to give than to receive, the five wise virgins realised that their giving of oil to the five foolish virgins would cost them by preventing their meeting with the bridegroom. Likewise, we should be able to distinguish a distraction from a real plea for help.

In the story of Elijah in *1 Kings 19:11*, we also see an example of someone that wasn't distracted:

> *[11]And he said, Go forth, and stand upon the mount before the LORD. And, behold, the LORD passed by,*

and a great and strong wind rent the mountains, and brake in pieces the rocks before the LORD; but the LORD was not in the wind: and after the wind an earthquake; but the LORD was not in the earthquake: 12And after the earthquake a fire; but the LORD was not in the fire: and after the fire a still small voice.

1 Kings 19:11-12

The breaking of a mountain, great wind, an earthquake, and a fire, could all be very distracting, especially when the answer is in a still small voice. Despite all of these things, Elijah was not distracted. In this situation, it would have been very easy to miss God, but Elijah passed the test.

In a situation where we go after our job from God, we need to be fully aware that there could be distractions. But we need to make up our minds that we will not be taken off course.

CHAPTER 13

Do not focus on the natural

*D*uring a period in my life when I was believing God for a job, God spoke these words to me. *"Do not look at the natural to determine what I am doing."*

At that point in my life, I was praying and holding on to the word of God, but nothing in the natural seemed to be working. When God spoke those words to me, it encouraged me to continually focus on the word while being aware that though I could see nothing moving in the natural, things were actually happening and being turned around in the supernatural.

What God said to me was in line with *2 Corinthians 4:18*

> [18]*While we look not at the things which are seen, but at the things which are not seen: for the things which are seen are temporal; but the things which are not seen are eternal.*
>
> *2 Corinthians 4:18*

I knew I had to focus on the word and not on the things around me. I wrote down the word that God spoke to me and stuck it on the dashboard in my car. Anytime any negative or discouraging thought crossed my mind, I focused on this word. It did not take long for me after that to get a job.

There is a story in the Bible that supports this point, which is that of Elisha and the King of Syria in *2 Kings 6:8*.

The King of Syria warred against Israel. Whenever he planned an attack, Israel was warned by Elisha (the man of God) of the impending danger. This is because Elisha was divinely informed by God and he, in turn, warned the King of Israel. This happened more than once. The King of Syria was troubled by the way the King of Israel got to know about all of Syria's plans. He was convinced that there was a spy amongst them until one of his generals told him that Elisha was the one responsible for telling the King of Israel what he (The King of Syria) talked about in his bedchamber.

In the natural world, without a spy or surveillance equipment, it is not possible for us to know what someone is saying in their bedchamber because we are not omnipresent. But Elisha was able to successfully warn the King of Israel.

The King of Syria then decided to send horses and chariots and a great army to capture Elisha at night. He thought that he would be able to catch Elisha unaware or off guard. The Syrian army then surrounded Elisha's house at night.

When Elisha's servant Gehazi went out in the

morning, he noticed that the Syrian army had surrounded the city. He ran back in and said to his master, "Alas, my master, what shall we do?"

Elisha answered, "*Fear not; for they that be with us are more than they that be with them.*" Gehazi was confused because he knew with certainty that it was just the two of them against the Syrian army. Elisha then prayed to God to open Gehazi's eyes. Gehazi then saw that the mountain was full of horses and chariots of fire round about Elisha. In the natural, no one could see the horses and chariots of fire that surrounded Elisha, but they were actually there. If Elisha had looked at what he saw in the natural, he would have been scared and given in, but he looked past what he could see with his natural eyes and into the spiritual realm to see his imminent victory. He would have been defeated if he had not looked with his spiritual eyes.

Likewise, we should not look at the natural and draw our conclusions based on what we can or cannot see. We should continually look at what the word of God is saying.

You may be looking for a job, and your situation may seem hopeless. It may seem as if there is no way out. You may have reached a dead end, or you may have peaked in your career. You may feel trapped and caged. In the natural, it seems as if the dream of ever coming out of the negative situation is an illusion or a mirage. Alternatively, you may even have a job, but you hate it passionately because you are not making progress. Promotion may be far from you, and you may have been bypassed for a promotion so many times that you have lost hope. Further, it could be that you are working at a job that is way below what you are qualified to do. The salary you are earning is just enough to keep you from sinking, or it could be that you are living from pay cheque to pay cheque.

I have good news for you. Stop looking at the natural to determine what God is doing. Start looking at the word of God. I pray that the God who opened Gehazi's eyes would open your eyes to see that he is working behind the scenes to give you your desired job.

Isaiah 55:6–11 says the following:

> *6Seek ye the LORD while he may be found, call ye upon him while he is near:*
> *7Let the wicked forsake his way, and the unrighteous man his thoughts: and let him return unto the LORD, and he will have mercy upon him; and to our God, for he will abundantly pardon.*
> *8For my thoughts are not your thoughts, neither are your ways my ways, saith the LORD.*
> *9For as the heavens are higher than the earth, so are my ways higher than your ways, and my thoughts than your thoughts.*
> *10For as the rain cometh down, and the snow from heaven, and returneth not thither, but watereth the earth, and maketh it bring forth and bud, that it may give seed to the sower, and bread to the eater:*
> *11So shall my word be that goeth forth out of my mouth:*

it shall not return unto me void, but it shall accomplish that which I please, and it shall prosper in the thing whereto I sent it.

Isaiah 55:6–11

You need to always remember that God's ways are much higher than your ways. He is able to do exceeding and abundantly above all that you can ever ask or think. He is not limited like you are. He has a million and one ways to get you that job. Put your trust in him, and let him bring his word to pass in your life.

God has said in *Mark 11:23,* "*Whatsoever you desire, when you pray, believe that you receive it and you shall have it.*" If you have prayed, then look into the spirit realm with your spiritual eyes and say you have it because God says you have it. The Syrian army could not defeat Elisha and Gehazi because God was with them. God is with you, and you will not be defeated.

CHAPTER 14

CAN GOD DO IT?

S ometimes, people hear the word of God. They hear other people's testimonies; they read the Bible or Christian books about how God helped someone get a fantastic job. But in their heart of hearts, they are saying, "Can God do it for me?", "Can I ever get such a testimony?", "My own case is different and peculiar," "My own story has a twist," "God is able, but can he really do anything about this situation?"

If you have asked yourself any one of these questions, you are not alone. Even the so-called mature Christians have asked themselves those questions at one time or the other.

In the Bible, it is recorded that Moses too questioned if God could do what he said he was going to do.

In *Numbers 11*, the Israelites were complaining that they were fed up of eating manna. Eating manna every day had become very monotonous, and they wanted to try something else. They wanted meat, but that was a difficult thing to ask for in the wilderness. The wilderness was full of sand, and in the natural, getting meat was impossible. Nobody was going to drop off meat in the wilderness. Even if they were, nobody could have enough meat to provide for the number of families in the camp. The situation looked impossible to both Moses and the people. Moses, out of his despondency and frustration, spoke to God. He said the following, as recounted in *Numbers 11:12–15*:

> *Have I conceived all this people? have I begotten them, that thou shouldest say unto me, Carry them in thy bosom, as a nursing father beareth the sucking child, unto the land which thou swarest unto their fathers? Whence should I have flesh to give unto all this people? for they weep unto me, saying, Give us flesh, that we may eat. I am not able to bear all this people alone, because it is too heavy for me. And if thou deal thus with me, kill me, I pray thee, out of hand, if I have found favour in thy sight; and let me not see my wretchedness.*
>
> *Numbers 11:12–15*

God replied that he was going to provide meat for them for a whole month. I believe Moses thought to himself, "Surely, God did not hear me" If he did, he would not promise to give all these people meat for a whole month. Maybe he has forgotten that we are in the wilderness.

Moses then spoke again (*Numbers 11:21–22*):

> *The people, among whom I am, are six hundred thousand footmen; and thou hast said, I will give them flesh, that they may eat a whole month. Shall the flocks and the herds be slain for them, to suffice them? or shall*

> *all the fish of the sea be gathered together for them, to*
> *suffice them.*
>
> *Numbers 11:21–22*

He tried to describe in greater detail the number of people who were in the wilderness, just in case God had forgotten. He took his time to explain to God that even if they decided to kill all the flocks and herds that were in the camp, they would still not have enough meat to feed the people. Did God really know what he was getting himself into? Was God aware of what he was promising? Could he really fulfil his promise? If not, it was not too late to back out.

God replied by asking Moses if his hand was too short to save. God then provided meat for the Israelites by causing the wind to blow and bring quails to the camp.

Likewise, are you looking for a job and asking yourself if God can do anything? Do you think your own situation is too peculiar for God to handle? Do you think you've exhausted all options? Do you think there is no logical way out of your complex job-hunting situation? Just as Moses asked God where he would get meat to feed 600,000 men, are you asking or wondering how God is going to deliver you out of this situation? Like the Israelites, do you think there is no way out? Are you murmuring and angry because you think you are stuck in your job and there is no way out?

Just as God replied to Moses, I believe God is saying to you, "Do you think my hand is too short that it cannot save?"

Just because you cannot see a way out does not mean there is no way out. There might be a limit to your own power, but there is no limit to the power of God. God knows more than a million and one ways to get you a job. He is not limited. Just as Moses tried to reason why God could not do it, do not try to reason why God would not be able to get you that job. Do not relegate God to your own level. The fact that you have exhausted all options does not mean that God too has exhausted all options. The Bible says his thoughts are not our thoughts and his ways are not our ways, as the heavens are higher than the earth, so are his ways higher than our ways and his thoughts higher than our thoughts.

We need to put our trust in him. We do not know how God is going to make it happen, but we do know that if we put our trust in him, he will not forsake or fail us.

Our mind may be shouting that there is no way out. It may also be saying that we have come to a dead end, a land of hopelessness and ill luck, but let us not accept this verdict. Let us believe the word of the Lord. Let us refuse to lean on our understanding and see God move on our behalf. The same God, who was able to feed 600,000 men, an unknown number of women, and children with meat for a whole month without asking anyone for help, is also able to give us a job that even surpasses our expectations. Let us believe this even when there is no logical way in the natural to get a job. Our God is able to perform what he has promised, so let us trust in him even when we can see no way out in the natural.

CHAPTER 15

ARE YOU GOING TO LET BAD EXPERIENCES STOP YOUR FAITH?

*J*ames was beheaded. The Church was praying that Peter would be released, as it was both Peter and James who were captured. Although they were praying that Peter would be released, there was an element of doubt in their prayer. They could not comprehend how God was going to save Peter.

We cannot predict how God is going to deliver us, but what we do know, is that God will come through for us.

Peter knocked on the door, and Rhoda went to the door thinking that perhaps another person had come to join the prayer meeting. To her amazement, it was Peter. She was shocked but also overjoyed. She rushed into the room where the disciples were still praying fervently; she interrupted their prayers by telling them that Peter was at the door. But no one believed her. They did not believe her because they did not imagine that God was going to deliver Peter that way.

We should never let our experience, whether good or bad, supersede what the word of God says.

> [5]*That your faith should not stand in the wisdom of men, but in the power of God.*
>
> *1 Corinthians 2:5*

I have seen God move in my life, mostly in the area of my job. I have believed God for jobs many times in the past and got them. Some other times, I thought I was walking in faith but maybe I was not, and I did not get the jobs. On moving to Canada from London, I knew I was in an unfamiliar territory. I had heard a lot of bad reports about how difficult it was for people to get jobs in Canada. To me, God is the same God, whether I am in London or in Canada. Your location is not an issue with him. I set my face like a flint and decided that I would get my job in Canada the same way I had got jobs in the past in London, England. I had heard stories of people fasting for 120 days just to get a job in Canada. I had heard about people spending months and even years trying to break into jobs in their chosen field. And here I was, without any Canadian experience which seemingly was crucial to getting a job in the country. It was not a question of whether God would come through for me or not. It was more a question of whether my faith would come through for me.

It was during this period of my life that the Lord led me to a message that challenged me. That message was in *Acts 12*.

Herod killed James, the brother of John, with a sword. In the earlier chapters of Acts, many powerful works had been done, so it was a shock to these Christians that James had been beheaded. Fear crept in, and their faith was being challenged. This execution was not the outcome they were expecting. What were they supposed to do? The Jews were pleased that James had been killed. The whole city knew and was in an atmosphere of jubilation. The news that one of the perpetrators had been caught and killed was everywhere. Because Herod saw that it pleased the Jews, he went on to take Peter. He put Peter in prison and delivered him to four quaternions (a group of four people – sixteen people) of soldiers.

This was a maximum security prison, and within that prison, he was kept under watch by sixteen soldiers.

On the night of his deliverance, he was sleeping between two soldiers and was bound with chains. He was put between two soldiers so that they could reinforce the security. All that could be done within the scope of the natural had been done to imprison and prevent him from escaping. There was no way he could naturally escape. He was in an inner cell in a maximum security prison. Tell me, in the natural, was there a way that Peter could have been delivered? What loophole had they not covered? What more could they have done in the natural to keep Peter from escaping than tying him with two padlocked chains, making him sleep between two soldiers, and leaving him under the charge of 16 soldiers?

They did everything possible naturally to stop him from escaping, but they forgot that the Bible says these words in *Psalm 127:1*

> *¹Except the LORD build the house, they labour in vain that build it: except the LORD keep the city, the watchman waketh but in vain.*
>
> *Psalm 127:1*

Or could it be that God caused the soldiers to fall asleep even though the King had made sure that he had enough to prevent all of them from falling asleep at the same time? It is only God who does not sleep or slumber.

> *⁴Behold, he that keepeth Israel shall neither slumber nor sleep.*
>
> *Psalm 121:4*

No matter what plan has been put in place to stop you from getting what you want, and no matter how secure it is, if God does not have a hand in it, it will fail. People can stop you from getting into the system, but they cannot stop God. They can secure things from you, but they cannot secure them from God. They might want to stop you from getting in, they might put roadblocks in your way, but they cannot stop God from getting you in. The Bible says that, they that know their God shall be strong and do exploits (Daniel 11:32). They can stop the natural man, but they cannot stop God. God can sneak you in to your desired job. If God could sneak Peter out of prison, then God can sneak people into jobs. If nothing could stop him from sneaking Peter out, then nothing can stop him from sneaking people in. Remember that it is God helping you and that you are not on your own.

> *13And Moses said unto the people, Fear ye not, stand still, and see the salvation of the LORD, which he will shew to you to day: for the Egyptians whom ye have seen to day, ye shall see them again no more for ever.*
> *14The LORD shall fight for you, and ye shall hold your peace.*
> *15And the Lord said unto Moses, Wherefore criest thou unto me? speak unto the children of Israel, that they go forward*
>
> *Exodus 14:13-15*

At face value, it looked like they had imprisoned Peter. It looked like no one could deliver him out of Herod's hand. Herod had done all he knew, but he did not know the scripture verse following from *Psalm 2:1–4*: which says

> *1Why do the nations conspire and the peoples plot in vain?*
> *2The kings of the earth set themselves, and the rulers take counsel together, against the LORD, and against his anointed, saying,*
> *3Let us break their bands asunder, and cast away their cords from us.*
> *4He that sitteth in the heavens shall laugh: the Lord shall have them in derision.*
>
> *Psalm 2:1–4*

I believe God was laughing at Herod. God was ridiculing him and making a mockery of him, as he thought 16 soldiers could stop God. He thought a maximum security prison, iron gates, bars, chains, and soldiers could stop God. They used all the man-made weapons they knew of, to hold Peter down. But God's weapons are greater and mightier than theirs. The supernatural is on a higher level than the natural. The natural is significantly less, and inferior to the supernatural. What you can see in the supernatural you cannot see in the natural, except when you look through the eyes of the spirit or through the word of God.

We must let the power of God work within us because we cannot please him if we do not have faith.

God sent one angel to the prison. The angel did not go through the door; the angel did not open the gate. The angel did not need to take permission from the sixteen soldiers, the prison guards, the prison warden, the gate men, and all those in authority in the natural realm.

The angel just walked into the prison, and the Bible recounts that light shined in the prison. The light shined, but it woke neither the two soldiers nor the remaining fourteen soldiers charged with keeping watch over Peter. The angel had to wake Peter up and say, "Arise up quickly." Did Peter need anyone to unfasten the chains? No, the chains just fell off. The angel then said, "Gird thyself and bind thy sandals, Cast thy garments about thee, and follow me."

Where were the two soldiers who were chained to Peter? Did they not hear when Peter put on his sandals and wore his clothes? Did they not hear when the angel spoke to Peter? Did they not hear the double chains drop? When chains drop, they make a loud noise. No matter how quietly you try to put metal on the floor, the clanging of metals together is loud. It could only be God who could make them sleep and not hear the metal chains drop.

How did Peter follow the angel? Even Peter thought it was a vision. What happened here is beyond human knowledge, wisdom, and understanding.

When Peter and the angel went past the first and second ward, they came to an iron gate that opened to them of its own accord. Is this natural? Have you ever heard of a locked gate opening of its own accord? They passed through this Iron Gate that opened for them and then went to another street, and then, the angel left. Peter then realised that he was not dreaming. He had been delivered by God's angel, but at that time, he thought he was dreaming. Peter then made his way to Mary's house. *Acts 12:15* says that those praying did not believe that Peter was at the door. Though they were praying for Peter's release, they were not expecting God to deliver him that way.

They may have expected that God would grant him favour with Herod and that maybe he would just be given a life sentence. They also thought that maybe he would be beaten and released or taken to court and later set free. But never in their wildest dreams did they think God would just send an angel to release Peter from prison.

Man cannot speak, and it comes to pass after God has spoken. It is only God who can speak after Man has spoken and can make it happen. Man did all he knew, to prevent Peter from leaving the prison, but that did not stop God. It was not a hindrance to God but an opportunity to show the fallible, unreliable, and undependable nature of man.

This was the same thing that happened when Jesus was put in the grave. They tried to make it secure. Though they could secure it from man, they could not secure it from God. He is God; he is not a man. He is our recourse, so we are truly helped by the only helper who no one can stop. If God is on a mission, we can say truly that it is a mission accomplished.

Although, those Christians knew that God could deliver Peter, they did not imagine that God would send an angel to deliver Peter. Similarly, it is recorded that Naaman too did not expect God to deliver him the way he was delivered (*2 Kings 5:14*).

Naaman went to Elisha for help because of his leprosy. He was angry because Elisha did not come out to him but just sent word that he should immerse himself in the dirty Jordan River seven times.

In verse 12, Naaman said, *"Are not Abana and Pharpar, rivers of Damascus, better than all the waters of Israel? May I not wash in them and be clean?"* So he turned and went away in a rage.

Sometimes, when we go to God with an issue, at the back of our minds, we have a pre-conceived idea about how God is going to deliver us.

So when the Christians met to pray for Peter's deliverance, it did not cross their minds that God could deliver Peter the way he did. These Christians wanted Herod to be merciful to Peter. They did not imagine that God could take Peter out of prison without Herod's consent. Others could have been praying for God to strike Herod dead before the morning, but God has the power to deliver his children from their enemy whether the enemy is dead or alive.

It is not for us to determine how God is going to do it. We should leave the doing to God and concentrate on the believing. We are to believe, and God will do what he has promised to do. For the Bible says in *Jeremiah 1:12*:

> *12 Then the LORD said to me, "You have seen well, for I am watching over my word to perform it."*
>
> *Jeremiah 1:12*

CHAPTER 16

Logic Will Fail

*I*n *Luke 5:4-7,* Peter and another fisherman were washing their nets. The act of washing nets is symbolic of them finishing for the day. Unfortunately, this was not a good day for Peter and his colleague because they caught nothing. They had tried and tried and concluded that they were not going to get anything that day. When you get to a point where you start packing up for the day, your whole body gets involved. You begin to tell yourself that it is over for today, that you cannot accomplish anything more in this area, and that you will try another day.

Just when they were packing up, Jesus got into their boat and preached to some other people. When he finished, he turned to Peter and his colleague and said to them, "Launch out into the deep, and let down your nets for a draught".

Peter had every reason to ignore Jesus. Jesus had seen him whilst he was washing his net. He did not tell him to stop, but he kept preaching. Peter could have reasoned by asking why Jesus had not stopped him from washing his net. Why did he have to wait till he finished preaching before speaking to him? Peter was a fisherman, and Jesus was a preacher. Peter was not just an ordinary fisherman; he was an experienced fisherman. He knew how to fish, when to fish and every trick in the book. He did not only know it, but he was very experienced. On this particular occasion, he had tried fishing and got nothing. Now Jesus, a preacher, was telling him to launch his nets out for a draught. In an understanding of the natural, this did not make sense. If Jesus had told him to go to another place to fish, it might have been a bit reasonable. But Jesus told him to try fishing in the same place where Peter had tried several times but to no avail.

Peter did not say, "I have already tried, and it did not work, so I am not going to try". Peter did not tell Jesus that there was no point. Peter instead said, "*Master, we have toiled all the night, and have taken nothing: nevertheless at thy word I will let down the net.*"

The Bible records that when they did what Jesus said, they caught *a great number of fish* and their nets broke.

You might be in a situation similar to that of Peter. You have sent out millions of resumes. You have applied for many jobs. You have attended many interviews. You have registered with many online agencies. You have applied in person. You have created many profiles with many organisations. You have done everything humanly possible, but you have got nothing.

You have picked up this book, and I am saying that you should believe in God for your job. What do you do? You don't want your hopes dashed because you know that you have tried everything. Just as Peter was told to throw his net into the same place that he had been fishing before, I am saying that you should take the word of God and apply for a job in the same saturated job market. Just as Peter had to throw away his logical reasoning and act on the word Jesus spoke to him, you too would have to throw away your logical reasoning and act on the word of God in the Bible.

Lay down your negative experiences and take hold of the word of God. Irrespective of what you have experienced or not experienced, take hold of the word of God and act on it. Peter had to let go of his negative experiences and his reasoning before acting on the word of God. You too will have to lay aside what you have experienced and act on the word again.

All you have to do is act on the word. It's as simple as that. You don't have to reason it out. Peter just acted. He did not reason that he had attempted and failed many times. If he had thought about it logically and tried to reason out how he could catch fish in a place where he had spent the whole day looking for fish, he would have missed it. If he had asked his colleague if what Jesus said made any sense, they would have talked themselves out of acting on the word

HOW TO FIND A JOB GOD'S WAY

because what Jesus said they should do did not make any sense. Sometimes, the word of God will make no sense to us, but we have to ignore our logic and go with the word of God alone. If you cannot explain logically how fish miraculously appeared in a place where someone had spent the whole day fishing and caught nothing, then you would not be able to figure out how God will get you a job in a saturated job market. So, instead of trying to rationalise or reason out how God is going to do it, just believe and leave God to do his work.

CHAPTER 17

WHAT YOU HAVE IS ENOUGH FOR GOD TO USE

⁶...for there is no restraint to the LORD to save by many or by few.

1 Samuel 14:6

*T*he above scripture infers that nothing can prevent God from helping us. Your minimal skillset is not a deterrent to God. God can work with whatever you have. It is not the number of qualifications or the years of experience that you have that makes it easy or difficult for God to help you. God can help whether you have a lot of experience or little of it or none at all.

If you are highly skilled with many years of experience, you would not think twice about asking God for a job that requires your skills. You would think that you have provided God with the tools that he needs to get the job done.

How about when you lack the necessary skills, can God still help? Can God help if you don't have any experience? Can God help if don't have the prerequisite skills required for the job?

Although God cannot be limited by what we have or do not have, he can be limited by our lack of faith (*Psalm 78:41*). *Hebrews 11:6* points out to us that we cannot please God if we lack faith.

I need to point out here that God can work with whatever skills you have, but you have a part to play in receiving what God has to offer

The scripture below says.

> [20]Now unto him that is able to do exceeding abundantly above all that we ask or think, according to the power that worketh in us.

> *Ephesians 3:20*

This means that, the power that works within us has a part to play in the exercising of our faith and the receiving of what God has for us. That is the reason why two people with exactly the same problem, will not necessarily get the same result. While one may successfully overcome the problem, the other may be broken and never get over the same. In Matthew 7:24–27, Jesus relates the story of two men who were faced with the same challenge; one came out victorious, and the other fell. One may ask, "What was the common denominator in the story of both men assuming that they both believed in God?" The common denominator was the challenge. The difference, however, was in how they acted and reacted to the challenge. This determined whether they succeeded or failed.

You can never get what you cannot see yourself having. If you think you are not good enough for the job, you will not get the job. The Bible says, *"As a man thinks in his heart so is he."* You can never rise above your thoughts. You can never attain a level that you cannot see yourself reaching. Where you are today is a reflection of what you thought about yesterday.

In the story of David and Goliath that I mentioned earlier, David visualised himself killing him before he actually did it. He would never have been able to kill Goliath had he not first seen himself killing him. David was convinced that he could defeat Goliath because he strongly believed in his covenant with God. He was conscious of the fact that God was with him and that God was going to help him defeat Goliath with whatever weapon he had. He did not focus on the strength of his weapons but on the might and bigness of his God.

Likewise, we should not focus on our skills but on the might and bigness of God.

David had five smooth stones, whereas Goliath had a big sword. In the natural, David was no match for Goliath and his armoury was also no match to Goliath's state-of-the-art sword. God backing David, however, gave David an edge over Goliath. God with us would give us an edge over and distinguish us from other candidates who merely put their trust in their skills.

The devil always tries to make us believe that God is limited when things don't add up in the natural.

Let's assume that the economy is bad and you are looking for a job. The devil would want to make you focus on the fact that the economy is bad and that you lack certain skills. He would try to milk the situation and intimidate you with it. Negative thoughts such as "Don't get your hopes high", "Scale down on your expectations", "Don't even bother trying", "You can never get a job in this economy", "Employers are laying people off and not recruiting" would keep bombarding your mind.

I would like to believe that David too had one or two such negative thoughts, which he shrugged off. Feed on negative thoughts, and they will destroy you. But feed on positive thoughts, and you will begin to see the light at the end of the tunnel. Just as the infestation of wood by termite starts on the inside, so also do negative thoughts start poisoning you slowly from the inside. Therefore, we should never give room to negative thoughts. Someone once said that you cannot stop birds from flying over your head, but you can stop them from building a nest on it. Negative thoughts will come, that is inevitable, but they do not need to take root in your heart. You should curtail and abort such thoughts before they become full-grown strongholds and take root in your heart. Never entertain negative thoughts for they will strangle your confidence and make you withdraw instead of giving the fight a shot.

To deal with these negative thoughts, you need to focus on the might of God. The more you focus on his might, the more insignificant and irrelevant the negative thoughts will be. When you focus on God, your lack of skills will become irrelevant in the grand scheme of things.

Abraham and Sara are examples of people who lacked what they needed to conceive a child. They had the promise from God, just as you and I have read a million and one promises in the Bible about God's provision. Despite that, everything looked bleak. Initially, they focused on what they did not have. Sara laughed when the angel told her that she was going to have a child (Genesis 18:12); she focused on her limitations and ignored the God factor. Abraham too did not need much persuasion to go into his wife's maid Haggai. He even had the guts to tell God that he should bless him through Ismael (Genesis 17:18) because he could not visualize how God could carry out such an impossible task.

Needless to say, they both got over this initial hurdle and focused on God. The outcome was their son Isaac, whose name means laughter *(Genesis 21:1–7)*. When they decided to look at God's word instead of their situation and circumstances, it took a turn for the good. Shifting your focus from what you do not have and putting it on God would definitely bring laughter into your life. The Bible is loaded with examples of people who had barely enough and got the equivalent of someone with much more. The miracle of the five loaves and two fishes proves this point.

A great multitude came to Jesus. They were with him for three days and had nothing to eat. The natural thing to do was to send the multitude away to get their own food, and that is what the disciples proposed. I believe they thought in their minds, "What are we going to do with this great number of people? There is no food or shop in this solitary place, the best thing to do is to send them away to get their own food". Jesus, however, did not see their location as a problem. He asked how many loaves they had, and he was told that it was just five loaves and two fish. In spite of being aware that this was insufficient, Jesus asked them to bring what they had. He blessed it and told them to distribute it. They all ate and were satisfied, and the disciples picked up twelve baskets of leftover food.

In the natural, it would have been impossible to feed five thousand with just five loaves and two fish. Jesus was not discouraged by the fact that he did not have enough bread or that the people were in an isolated place. He rather knew that God was able to use what he had. He knew that the little he had could be turned into a lot in the hands of his father.

If God could use the five loaves and two fish to feed five thousand, he can use whatever you have to get you a job. All you have to do is raise what you have to him, thank him for it, and believe that he would use it to get you that desired job.

Take your mind off what you do not have and instead focus on the might of God.

The miracle performed by Jesus of turning water into wine is another example where what the person had was not enough in the natural.

At Cana of Galilea, they ran out of wine at a wedding. It was not practical for them to go out and get more wine. Jesus was present at the wedding and asked them to fill water pots with water, draw out of it, and present it to the governor. They wanted wine, but they only had water. However, Jesus was able to use what they had to produce what they wanted. He did not say, "It is impossible". He rather told them what to do; they obeyed and got results.

I have been to interviews for certain positions in the past for which I did not have all the skills required. Despite falling short, the interviewers still offered me the job and told me that I could come in and learn. When you put your trust in God, he will make the little you have enough for what you want.

CHAPTER 18

ENCOURAGE YOURSELF WITH THE GOD FACTOR

*E*ncouraging yourself is something you should regularly do when going through challenges. As well-meaning as friends and associates can be in being a source of encouragement, the best encouragement you can get is the one you give yourself. As we saw in the previous chapter, despising the small things you have around you could mean that you are trying to "tell" God how to bring things to pass in your life. God has more ways than our minds can conceive.

Whenever I find myself looking for a job, I find stories from the Bible that paint a picture of the might of God in operation. Let me share one of such stories with you.

In 2 *Kings* 6, Samaria was besieged by Syria. No one could enter or leave the city and they started running out of food. In no time, there was a severe famine and food was scarce and expensive. People were starving and desperate. In fact, some people started eating their children.

One day, as the King of Israel was passing by, he was told about the story of women that had started eating their children. He was so angry and frustrated that he blamed the calamity that was happening on Elisha. He then vowed to behead Elisha. The king and his servants then headed to Elisha's house.

When they got there, Elisha said, *"Hear ye the word of the Lord; thus says the Lord, Tomorrow about this time shall a measure of fine flour be sold for a shekel, and two measures of barley for a shekel, in the gate of Samaria."* This word was mocked by one of the king's officers. In today's language, he could be termed as the special adviser to the king. He was a very bright and knowledgeable man. He disagreed with what Elisha said and said *"If the Lord would make windows in heaven, might this thing be?"* In other words, the probability of this happening was impossible. Elisha then replied him that *"Thou shalt see it with thine eyes, but shalt not eat thereof."*

That night, four destitute lepers that were sitting at the entrance of the gate, having not been allowed in as a result of their leprosy decided to surrender to the enemy rather than starve to death. They reasoned that perhaps the Syrians would allow them to live.

To their surprise, when they got to the Syrian camp, there was no one there. During the night, God had caused the Syrian army to hear a great noise that sounded like horses, chariots and a great army. The Syrians thought the king of Israel had hired soldiers to come and fight against them. So they fled, leaving everything they had.

ENCOURAGE YOURSELF WITH THE GOD FACTOR

The lepers then went from one tent to another, eating and taking gold, silver and whatever they could take. Then they said, we need to inform our King, we cannot keep this great information to ourselves. How much can we eat anyway? This is a great day, let us go and tell the King. To cut a long story short, the King was informed, at first, he did not believe and thought it was just a trick that was being played by the Syrians to lure them into coming out of Samaria in search of food. But then they decided that they had nothing to lose by sending a few people to check out if it was infact true that the Syrians had left everything and fled in terror. It was confirmed that this was true. Everyone in the city was informed, they all ran out to Syria to get food. The word of God that was spoken by Elisha came to pass, and the special adviser that doubted was trampled upon as people were trying to rush out of Samaria to get some food from Syria. The man saw Elisha's prediction come to pass, but he did not taste out of it. He died while Elisha's words and predictions came to pass.

In the natural, it was an impossible situation, and there was no way that the word Elisha spoke could come to pass. Because of this, the officer (analyst/professional) on whose hand the King leant said, *"Behold, if The Lord would make windows in heaven, might this thing be?"* He decided to lean on his understanding, looked at the situation around him, analysed it, and compared it to the trends. He then concluded that based on his analysis and comparison, it was impossible for Elisha's words to happen. He did not consider God, the maker of heavens and the earth who is everywhere at the same time. This God is the one who speaks and whose word never returns unto him empty, the one who opens the door that no man can shut. The Analyst leaned on his understanding instead of trusting in God. It is true that Elisha's answer did not seem to add up to the situation at hand, but there is a God in heaven who has a hand in the affairs of men and causes things to work out the way he wants when men put their trust in him.

This God lives is a realm beyond the natural one, called the supernatural realm. Whether you believe it or not, this realm affects and controls what happens in the natural. Once Elisha gave the word from God, things had to be moved in the supernatural to make what Elisha said come to pass. The natural always aligns with what is happening in the supernatural, but most of us are oblivious to this fact because we have been trained to react and respond to what we see, feel, or hear.

When God gives a word, we need to take that word and hold on to it no matter how foolish it seems. There may be a huge difference between our situation and the word that we are standing on. It might even be as different as night and day, but God is still God, and nothing can stop him.

In this particular story, many things could have

turned out differently, but everything happened the way they did because God was moving behind the scenes. It is just like watching a play in the theatre, you cannot see what is happening behind the scenes. You can see the actors performing but not those behind the curtains. While the actors are performing, there are other things happening behind the scenes. For example, people run around in the background doing things and making sure that the performance goes smoothly.

Life is exactly like that. There are so many things happening in the unseen realm, orchestrating the way things happen in the natural realm. The fact that we cannot see these things does not mean they are not there. It only means that we cannot see them from the realm that we are operating in.

The four lepers mentioned in the story could have stayed at the gate begging, but they said, *"Why sit we here until we die?"* This was not a coincidence. Why didn't they ask this question two weeks before that day? That was not their first day at the gate. They had been at the gate for some time. Why did they decide to go to Syria the day the man of God said, *"Hear ye the word of The Lord; thus saith The Lord, Tomorrow about this time…"*? Did anyone cajole them to go to Syria? They knew the risk they were taking by going to Syria, but they still decided to go. It was because they were being moved by supernatural forces which they were unaware of.

When they got to the camp of Syria, there was

no one there. The Syrians could have still been there if God had not made them hear the noise of chariots and horses, even the noise of a great army.

The Syrians could have heard the noise and decided to really confirm that an army was coming to fight against them before they fled, but they did not. They just ran. Why did they do so? They ran because God made them believe what he wanted them to believe. God is capable of making people see things the way he wants them to see it. Likewise, the lepers could have decided not to tell anyone in Samaria. Instead, they went back. Why? They went back because that is what God wanted. The word could have got to the palace, and the officers could have prevented that word from reaching the King. The King and his officials could have discarded it as nonsense, but they did not. Their word was supposed to get to the King for him to decide that the Samaritans should go to Syria. This also happened because God's word can never fail

> [34] My covenant will I not break, nor alter the thing that is gone out of my lips.
>
> *Psalm 89:34*

When the word got to the King, the King too could have dismissed it. It is obvious that the King did not believe it. He could have decided that no one should go to Syria. But again, he allowed them to check it out. The King too did not know that he was being controlled by the supernatural. They were just fulfilling the prophecy given by the man of God. So many things could have gone wrong and prevented the word from coming to pass, but God is God, and his word can never fail. We need to hold on to his word and not make our final decisions or assumptions based on what we see, feel or hear.

CHAPTER 19

PERSEVERE

¹⁸And, behold, men brought in a bed a man which was taken with a palsy: and they sought means to bring him in, and to lay him before him.
¹⁹And when they could not find by what way they might bring him in because of the multitude, they went upon the housetop, and let him down through the tiling with his couch into the midst before Jesus.

Luke 5:18–19 (KJV)

¹⁸And behold, some men were bringing on a bed a man who was paralyzed, and they were seeking to bring him in and lay him before Jesus,
¹⁹but finding no way to bring him in, because of the crowd, they went up on the roof and let him down with his bed through the tiles into the midst before Jesus.

Luke 5:18–19 (ESV)

These men had a friend who was paralysed. He could not do anything by himself, as he was indisposed. They decided to carry him to Jesus. On getting there, they saw that they could not get in, as there were hindrances. There was a crowd of people and no way of carrying a paralytic man through the crowd. There was also a lot of shoving and pushing, and it was easier to turn back than go forward. The men had come this far and were faced with a seemingly challenging situation. How on earth were they supposed to get past the crowd with a paralytic friend?

Many would have given up and turned back. Their paralysed friend would not have complained if they turned back. He would have understood that they had done their best, but turning back was not an option for them. Instead, they decided to go a different route.

There was no way of reaching Jesus by going through the crowd, so they decided to climb to the top of the house, remove the tiles from the roof, and lower their friend to Jesus. They did whatever it took to get Jesus's attention. Their perseverance ultimately paid off because Jesus healed their friend.

Sometimes, when we are out of work, in between contracts or just trying to get into the job market, our situation could be likened to that of the paralytic man. We are paralysed, helpless, and hopeless. We need friends to prop us up. The job market is overcrowded, and we cannot see a way out through the millions of people who are also looking for jobs. The situation looks gloomy. We cannot see how we will stand out in such a saturated market. There is a lot of stampeding for the very few jobs available. There are many people who are more qualified. They have better and more relevant experiences. Additionally, they are already in the system.

When your situation is like that described above, like the friend of the paralytic man, you must persevere. You must do all you know to do. You must not take the path of least resistance. You must leave no stone unturned. Ecclesiastes 11:4 advises us not to wait for the situation to be perfect before we step out.

> [4]He who observes the wind will not sow and he who regards the clouds will not reap.
>
> *Ecclesiastes 11:4 (ESV)*

> [4]Farmers who wait for perfect weather never plant. If they watch every cloud, they never harvest.
>
> *Ecclesiastes 11:4 (NLT)*

If the friend of the paralytic had said, "Let us go back home and come back when it is less busy", they may never have got their desired outcome. Although they acted when the condition was less favourable, they still got what they wanted.

There is no perfect time to get a job. So stop waiting for the perfect conditions before applying for a job. You can get a job during hard times, when employers are laying people off, when the economy is bad, or at any other unfavourable time. There will always be a reason why it is not the best time to apply for a job. There will always be something not quite right or an element of doubt lurking in the back of our minds when we decide to launch out.

Did the paralytic man's friend take him to Jesus

at the wrong time? No, because there is no right or wrong time.

Some people might say, "Don't apply in December because most people will be on holiday". Others may say, "Don't apply when the organisation has almost finished spending their budget". Some of you can testify that you know people who got jobs in December and March. Therefore, you can apply anytime. The writer of Ecclesiastes says that if you observe the wind, you will not sow. We should sow or launch out whenever we want because we do not know which application would get us the job.

Negative thoughts and doubts will definitely come, but we need to doubt those doubts and press forward. What if we apply and get rejected? It is better to try and fail than not to try at all. If you try, you at least have a 50% chance of getting it. If you do not apply, you already have a 0% chance of getting in. However, if you fail, you can at least see it as an experience under your belt. Learn from that experience and move on. Never stop trying. Just because you were rejected by 120 people does not mean you will be rejected by the 121st person.

There is a poem I found on the internet that I like reading. This poem encourages me to persevere and not give up.

Don't Quit (Author Unknown)

[1]When things go wrong, as they sometimes will,

When the road you're trudging seems all uphill,

When the funds are low and the debts are high,

And you want to smile, but you have to sigh,

When care is pressing you down a bit-

Rest if you must, but don't you quit.

Life is queer with its twists and turns,

As every one of us sometimes learns,

And many a fellow turns about

When he might have won had he stuck it out.

Don't give up though the pace seems slow -

You may succeed with another blow.

Often the goal is nearer than

It seems to a faint and faltering man;

Often the struggler has given up

When he might have captured the victor's cup;

And he learned too late when the night came down,

How close he was to the golden crown.

Success is failure turned inside out -

The silver tint in the clouds of doubt,

And you never can tell how close you are,

It might be near when it seems afar;

So stick to the fight when you're hardest hit -

It's when things seem worst that you must not quit.

---

1 Accesed at http://www.ellenbailey.com/poems/ellen_099.htm on 20th July 2017.

CHAPTER 20

WHILE YOU ARE WAITING GOD IS
WORKING

31But they that wait upon the LORD shall renew their strength; they shall mount up with wings as eagles; they shall run, and not be weary; and they shall walk, and not faint.

Isaiah 40: 31

Waiting, as defined by Dictionary.com means *to remain inactive or in a state of repose, until something expected happens.* In Hebrew, it means *to hope for, to anticipate.*

Most of us don't like to wait, but waiting is a part of life. We wait in line to pay at the grocery shop; we wait to be served at the restaurant; we wait outside schools to pick up our children; we wait for taxis, and we wait for our turn at the bank. Everybody has to wait for something every day.

The longer the waiting process, the more impatient, restless, and frustrated we sometimes get. I haven't come across anyone who loves waiting. In fact, many people try to devise means of cutting down the waiting time. Hence the need of the fast food industry. This industry has cut the waiting time for our food to next to nothing, though the food is not as delicious as properly made food.

We are always rushing to the next place or thing, and we have no time to remain motionless. Instant gratification is the order of the day and patience is no longer seen as a virtue.

The same thing applies when we are waiting for the manifestation of our jobs. When we pray to God for our jobs, we want him to answer immediately. We don't really have the time to wait. We've got bills to pay, children's fees to pay, career ladders to climb, and we just do not have the time to wait around. Also, other people are moving ahead so it seems unfair that we should be in a state of stagnation.

Waiting around is always seen as a negative. During periods of waiting, it seems as if there is no movement in our lives. Things seem stagnant, and an element of uncertainty looms around us. By waiting around, we feel we are wasting precious time.

All through the Bible, there are examples of people who had to wait for God. Moses had to wait for God to reveal his assignment in life. Abraham and Sara had to wait for God to give them their promised child. Joseph had to wait till God delivered him from prison. Others that had to wait were Daniel, the Israelites, David, Jacob and the list could go on and on.

Why did God not deliver these people immediately? Why did he have to make them wait? Surely, he is God, and he can do all things, so why waste time and make them wait?

Some of the reasons why God makes us wait are as follows:

To develop character in us
While waiting, we have time to examine ourselves and look inwards. We have the time to notice the things in our lives that are not right and correct them. We can ask ourselves if there is anything in our lives that is preventing us from getting what we have asked God for. We learn through times of uncertainty.

Moses had to wait for 40 years before God used him. In those 40 years, he was transformed from a man who went out to kill someone to one who learnt to wait on God and listen for instructions.

In my own life, I have noticed that it is during periods of waiting that I have grown most as a Christian. It is during those uncomfortable times that I have had the time to seek God more, pray more, read my Bible more, and seek his face for guidance and direction. As I did that, I became quiet in my spirit to hear what God wanted me to change in my life.

To reveal our motives
Waiting reveals our true motives. God

always weighs our actions (*1 Samuel 2:3*), but sometimes, we are oblivious to the real reason why we want something. We ask and receive not because we ask amiss to satisfy our lusts (*James 4:3*). During periods of waiting, we realise that we need to pay a price for what we want. Are you really desperate enough to pay that price, or do you just want it to boost your ego? If you want it for the latter, you would not be willing to pay the price to get it when things get tough. Some people want good jobs so that they can boast to their friends that they are big and important people. Some want better houses so they can show off to their family members that they have made it. Other people just want to stand out. All these motives are wrong. Wanting a job to pay your bills or take care of your family are better reasons. No one would condemn you for wanting to take better care of your family. But wanting to show off that you are better than others or that you can afford that bigger and better car is not right. Waiting will sometimes make us look inward and reveal the true reason why we want the job we have asked God for.

Waiting reveals our selfishness and the fact that we are not truly seeking God the giver, but the gift we can get from him. We say we are worshipping God, but all we want is what he has and not a true relationship with him. Waiting will reveal our true motives for seeking him. While waiting, we could say one of two things. We could say "If I do not get it, I will not seek God anymore. He has not supplied my need, so I do not believe him "or we could have the attitude that even if God does not do it, we will still serve him and trust him. The correct approach is the latter.

We might not understand why we have not received our job from Him, but we trust Him and know that everything will work out well for our good. The person that is after what he or she can get, will be ready to quit and quick to look for alternative compromising ways. But the one that is truly waiting on God, will not give up.

The Bible tells us of the story of the Israelites as they journeyed from Egypt to the Promised Land. This journey was supposed to take the Israelites at most forty days but it took them forty years. There were twelve tribes of Israel. One of the tribes of Israel decided to settle for second best because the trip was taking too long. When they got to the land of Jazer, they were satisfied and decided not to continue the journey to the Promised Land. The other eleven tribes of Israel continued the journey (*Numbers 32:1-33*). Waiting revealed how much they were willing to endure to get what they wanted.

The sons of Reuben were not willing to continue the journey.

Waiting separates those who genuinely want something from those who are not in the game for the long haul.

To give things to us at the right time because he sees the bigger picture

God sees the bigger picture. He knows the end from the beginning. He has the bird's eye view. He knows the right time to give us what we need. He sees all the pieces of the puzzle, while we only see a piece. We need to trust God during those difficult times and believe that he knows the right time and would give us that job at the appointed time. God knows the best time to launch us out. He knows the best job to give to us. We might be going after a certain job when God knows that if we wait for a couple of weeks, a better one would be available. He could be moving someone out of a job right now to get us there. He could be making someone relocate to put us in that position. He could be creating opportunities for a position to open for us while you are waiting. Things are definitely happening in the spiritual realm.

Alternatively, it could be that if God gives it to us too early, we might mess things up. Moses nearly messed things up by killing the Egyptian; he had to go into hiding for 40 years.

When Moses was born, his mother had to hide him for three months. During that time, I am sure there were a million and one thoughts telling her that her son would be found and killed. God made his sister leave him in the water, and he also led Pharaoh's daughter to pick him up because God wanted him to get a good education, learn proper etiquette in the palace, and develop the leadership skills that he was going to need to lead the Israelites out of Egypt. There are things and skills that we learn during our periods of waiting that we would never learn otherwise.

In the story of Joseph in the Bible, if the Butler had remembered Joseph as soon as he got out of prison, Joseph would not have been in the prison to interpret Pharaoh's dream and he would not have been the Prime Minister. If his brothers had not sold him into slavery, he wouldn't have been in Egypt. All the mishaps that he experienced were all part of God's bigger plan. They were a part of the bigger picture that Joseph did not see.

To help us develop patience

Waiting helps us develop patience. Patience is a virtue. It makes you steadfast in the face of adversity. It has a part to play in our faith walk (James 1:2–4) so that we may be perfect and lack nothing. Faith and patience go hand in hand. They are twin virtues that you need to hold on to in order to get what you want from God.

Impatience makes people do silly things that they later regret.

Esau sold his birth right to Jacob because he could not wait patiently. He was hungry; he wanted food, and he wanted it immediately. He was not prepared to wait. He was willing to trade what he had to get what he wanted. He later regretted his actions.

In *2 Kings 6,* the Bible tells us about two women who decided to kill their children because the famine was so severe. Had they waited a few more days, one of them would not have lost her son. I can imagine how hard it must have been for her to go through life, knowing that, had she waited a few more days, she would have still had her only child.

We need to remember that God is patient with us as well. God waits patiently for many years, giving us a long rope to pull, to see us change that bad habit. We miss things and make mistakes so many times, but he does not give up on us. Instead, he waits steadfastly, till we turn a new leaf.

The next time we try to rush into the next job or promotion and find ourselves waiting impatiently and worrying, let us remember that God is not slack concerning his promises. He knows what he is doing and will give us our desired job at the appointed time. He always makes all things beautiful in his time (*Ecclesiastes 3:11*).

Let us keep our eyes on the goal and endure with patience the race that is set before us (*Hebrews 12:1*). Let us remember that if we wait patiently, we will get our desired goal.

To make us depend on him

When we come to the end of ourselves, we always look to God for help. Waiting makes us realise that we have no strength against the battle we are facing, and it also forces us to look to God for help. It forces us to rely on God for strength. When things are rosy, and we lack nothing, we rush around, get busy for nothing, and sometimes forget God. But when we encounter a mountain that we cannot cross, we immediately remember God and rush to him for help. Waiting has the ability to help us focus on God. In our quest for help, we always have no alternative but to look to the omniscient and omnipotent God for help. It takes us to the place that we should have been in the first place. It takes us to the presence of God.

Hannah waited on God to grant her a child *(1 Samuel 1:20)*. Her situation of having borne no children drew her to the presence of God for help.

Hezekiah ran to God for help when he received a letter from the King of Assyria *(2 Kings 19:14–19)*.

One should never confuse waiting with the lack of motion. While we are waiting, we need to understand that God is working behind the scenes and things are happening in the unseen realm.

A good analogy is that of the Chinese bamboo tree. The Chinese bamboo tree requires the same amount of nurturing as any other normal tree. It requires water, sunshine, and fertile soil. While other trees start growing and budding, there is virtually no visible sign of activity in the life of this tree for four solid years. During this time, the farmer would have to exercise faith, patience, and perseverance.

In the fifth year, the Chinese bamboo tree grows an extraordinary 90 feet in the space of five weeks.

How did the tree grow 90 feet in just five weeks?

The answer lies in the solid root system of this tree. This tree grows and develops its root system for four long years so that it can support the structure and weight that the tree would eventually reach. The root grows deep and wide while spreading and rooting itself firmly in the ground in preparation of the weight and height it would eventually grow to. The root also enables it to withstand harsh conditions for many years.

What if the farmer decided to uproot the tree after a year, by thinking that his watering and nurturing were a waste of time? What if he did this by not realising that although he could not see anything above the ground, something was actually happening underground?

We need to take a lesson or two from this tree. When we are waiting on God for the manifestation of our job, though nothing is visible, something is actually happening behind the scenes. While you are waiting, God is actually working.

Of course, when we decide not to wait, there will always be consequences, and most of the time the consequences are painful, and the effects may last a lifetime. Let me give some examples.

We create unnecessary problems

When we decide that God is taking his time and we decide to do things ourselves, we complicate issues and get lumbered with unnecessary problems that could have been avoided if we had waited for God. In the story of Abraham and Sarah, Sarah convinced Abraham to have a child with her maid. This later aggravated her till she decided to give Abraham an ultimatum to either get rid of her maid and the child or risk losing her. The descendants of that child, Ismael, are now known to be enemies of the Israelites.

Our wrong decisions create shameful situations

When you take things into your own hands, you end up being ashamed. God can see what you cannot see and knows the right time. Running off at a premature time only leads to shame and embarrassment. The prodigal son in the Bible could not wait for the death of his father before receiving his inheritance. He was given the money which he squandered with people whom he thought were friends. He soon ran out of money and had to do jobs that he would never have dared doing if he had waited for the right time. It got so bad that he had to eat food given to pigs. He realised his mistake and had to eat his humble pie and go back to his father. He was so ashamed of himself and for what he did. His father, however, took him back with open arms. Running ahead of God will only lead to shame and disgrace.

What we get will never be as good as what we should have waited for

God is always right so if you run ahead of him, you will always get it wrong and come back to him. The story of the prodigal son highlights this.

We compromise

Not waiting on God will lead to compromise and what you compromise to get, you will lose.

You step out of God's will into a place of danger

By running ahead of God, you remove yourself from under his protection and leave yourself open to the attack of the devil.

Broken fellowship

Like the prodigal son, you stray away from your father and would not hear him clearly.

You settle for second best

Like Abraham, you have an Ismael (son from the maid) instead of an Isaac (promised child from God).

CHAPTER 21

DON'T SHORT-CIRUIT YOUR BREAKTHROUGH

*A*n interesting and exciting part of the job hunting process is when things begin to happen. The agent calls you and tells you that an employer is interested in having a face-to-face interview with you. You've been shortlisted for an interview. You are excited. Your prayer seems to be working.

Before you jump around and start telling everybody that you've been shortlisted, hold on. This is the time to focus more on the word of God than on things that are happening around you. You need to prepare for the interview, but you also need to stay focused on the word of God that you are holding on to. It is very easy at times like this to let go of the word and focus on the so-called things that we see happening in the natural, but we need to realise that if we let the word slip, we might short-circuit our miracle.

Many people have short-circuited their miracles by taking their eyes off the word too early and putting it on the things that they see. You do not want a half-baked miracle.

Many years ago, I applied for a job and was called for an interview. I prepared for the interview and actually saw the hand of God move in my life during the preparation stage. On the day of the interview, I came across a technical term in my field of expertise, which I had never heard about and read up on it. During the interview, I was asked about that topic, and I answered the question very well. I also answered the other questions well. The interviewers had told me before I left that they were impressed with me and hinted that they were looking to offer me the job. They sent me off to the Human Resources Manager just to fill out some forms and go through the last stage, which they said was just a formality. They had even called the Director to come and chat with me because they were keen on hiring me.

On getting home, I shared what happened with a lady who was staying with me at that time. I told her about how I had miraculously come across this technical term, read about it, and answered the question asked brilliantly. Unknowingly to me, I took my eyes off the word and was consumed and focused on all that was happening. Things were taking shape and looking pretty good. I was basking in the glory of how the interview went.

The next day, I was so excited as I waited anxiously for the call from the agent to tell me that I had been hired for the job. But, I was flabbergasted when the agent told me that I did not get the job because the HR Manager said he had a gut feeling that it was not going to work.

I had passed the interview; I had passed the technical screening; I was told in the interview that I was going to be hired, but I was not hired because someone had a gut feeling it was not going to work out.

I took a step back and tried to see where I had missed it. It was then that I realised I had taken my eyes off the word because of the positive things that were happening. I learnt a big lesson that I should never take my eyes off the word till I actually get the job. Our rejoicing should always be based on the word and not on physical things (*John 20:29*).

When you take your eyes off the word of God and focus on things in the natural realm, you are susceptible to the devil's devices. Once the devil notices that you have taken your eyes off the word, he can manipulate things around you to further distract you. The devil can use both good and bad things to distract us.

It is more common for people to focus on the word when things are not happening and when they have not yet seen any positive manifestation. I always believe that the most delicate part of my walk of faith while believing God for a job is when I start seeing little positive signs that things are working out. During times when I can see a little light at the end of the tunnel, I am always very careful to focus more on the word and not on the sign so that I don't act based on what I can see instead of based on the word. At times like this, you must be careful not to have the "act of faith" but the "true faith" which believes based on what the word of God says and not on evidence seen or unseen. You cannot afford to take your eyes off the word until you have the full manifestation of your job.

An example of someone who started out in faith and later got distracted by things happening around him can be found in *Matthew 14:25*.

Peter was in a boat with some other disciples. They saw someone walking on water, and they were scared. Jesus told them that he was the one walking on water and that there was no need for them to be afraid. Peter then answered, "*Lord if it be thou, bid me come unto thee on the water.*" Jesus told him to come. Without thinking, Peter took a leap of faith and walked on water. Then, he saw the boisterous wind and took his eyes off Jesus. As soon as he did this, he began to sink. Before Peter sank, he experienced the miraculous. He actually walked on water. You might say that the boisterous wind was a negative experience and not a positive one. Irrespective of whether what you see is negative or positive, if you take your eyes off the word and instead focus on signs and wonders, you will sink.

The Bible encourages us in *Hebrews 12:2* to, look unto Jesus, the author and finisher of our faith. Jesus is the word of God (*1 John 1:1*) so we could say that the Bible encourages us to continually look at the word. *Revelations 2:25* also instructs us to hold onto what we have till it manifests. Before our job materialises, what we have is the word of God, and we are instructed to hold onto the word till we get our job.

Revelations 2:25 says the following:

> [25]*But that which ye have already hold fast till I come.*
>
> *Revelations 2:25*

CHAPTER 22

THE ONUS IS ON YOU

I remember when I first came to Canada and was looking for a job. Everything seemed hard and impossible. Nothing seemed to be working. The job market in Canada seemed dead compared to the one I was used to in the UK.

I kept praying, reading the word and saying the right things. I was doing all I knew to do, but had very little feedback. I knew things had to be happening in the spiritual realm, but not much was happening in the natural.

It was during this period that God spoke a word to my heart. He said to me, *"Do not look at the natural to determine what I am doing."* I took that word, wrote it on a sticky note, and stuck it in my car close to the steering wheel. I did that to continually remind myself that though things looked grim in the natural, it did not necessarily reflect what was going on in the spiritual realm.

We need to realise that it takes time for the natural to catch up with and reflect what is happening in the spiritual realm. The spiritual realm is more real than the natural realm, and we cannot connect to it with our five senses. We need to hold on and not cave in.

Someone said, "*Life does not work by chance, it works by choices*", and that is really true if we take the time to mull over that sentence. What our life has turned out to be today is an accumulation of the choices we made yesterday.

You cannot wake up one morning and find yourself where you have not planned to be.

Someone I know told me about one of their roommates in university. This person kept playing video games every night and paid very little attention to his school work. Of course, this reflected in his grades because he always scored bad marks. What puzzled them was that he was always shocked about his grades and did not understand why he did not do well. He claimed that he attended lectures, but that was not all he needed to do. He also needed to go over his lecture notes and make sure he was ready for tests instead of spending a lot of time on things for which he was not going to be tested on.

Likewise, in life, we need to make choices that would propel us towards the goals that we want to achieve. If you want to get a job by faith, then you have to spend time in the word of God, in prayer, and fellowship with God. You will also have to spend some time studying and bringing yourself up to speed in your chosen field. Learn about new technology, read books, and do all you need to do. Do what you can do and leave the rest to God, but make sure you are doing something and not just being lazy. Make good choices, and do not spend all your time watching television or being on social media. If these things are stealing away your valuable time, then schedule a time to watch television and be on social media. But make sure that you give more time to what is important to you. Give more time to the word of God, prayer, praise and also give time for self-improvement.

We should never major on the minor and minor on the major. Spend more time on things that are major to you, tailor your choices towards the major things in life. And spend less time on the minor things in life such as catching up with old friends on Facebook and watching YouTube videos that entertain you. There is no harm in spending time on these things, but just make sure you are allocating the correct amount of time to them. Spending 12 hours watching movies is an overkill. You do not need a prophet to tell you that you are killing and wasting time. Make good choices daily, and remember that life does not work by chance but by the choices we make.

The Bible spells this out clearly in *Deuteronomy 30:19*:

> [19]I call heaven and earth to record this day against you, that I have set before you life and death, blessing and cursing: therefore choose life, that both thou and thy seed may live.

Deuteronomy 30:19

Page | 165

The Bible is encouraging us to choose life and do things God's way instead of doing things our own way. A choice is an act of selecting or deciding when faced with two or more possibilities. For every second we spend on earth, we make at least one choice. The choice to stay where we are or the choice to do something different; the choice to eat something healthy or the choice to eat what we want; the choice to spend our time the way we want or the choice to invest it on something that is worthwhile in the future. Indeed, the onus is on us.

Success is indeed predictable. Deuteronomy 30:19 tells us we have choices to make and *Joshua 1:8* encourages us to follow these practices:

- *Meditate on the word day and night*
- *Observe all that is written therein*

If you do these, you shall make your way prosperous and succeed.

Can you see then that success is predictable? Did you notice that the scripture did not mention anywhere that your teacher, your professor, your mother, your father, your relatives, your husband, your children, or anyone else would make you successful? It specifically says that you will make your own way prosperous and have good success.

Another thing that comes to mind is the fact that some people keep doing the same thing every day without getting any result. They never even give a thought to changing something to get a different result. If you have been at the same spot for five years without seeing any change, is it not time for you to look within to see if there is something that you need to change to get a different result? It is a no-brainer that what you are getting out of life is commensurate to what you are putting into it. If you are not satisfied with where you are, then do something. Make a choice towards what you are looking to get out of life instead of waiting for some chance.

Evaluate your life and cut out things that would not take you to your desired destination.

That is the same with life. If we see that what we are doing in life is always leading us to a roadblock, we need to take a different route so that we can arrive at our destination. Staying at the same place for ten years will not take us to our destination. Taking stock and deciding on a new route would get us to where we are heading.

People who are successful can attest to the fact that their success is due to the choices they have made.

> [29]Have you seen a man that is diligent in his business? He would stand before kings and not before mean men.
>
> Proverbs 22:29

In concluding this chapter, I would like to share a story in the Bible about an unjust servant who decided to turn an unfavourable situation into a favourable one. He knew the onus to succeed was on him and not on his master. *(Luke 16:8)*

This servant was accused of wasting his master's goods. His master made up his mind to get rid of this servant, but before the master could get rid of him, he decided to call his master's debtors and write off part of each debtor's debt. He inevitably collected some of the debt his master might never have been able to collect. He did this in the hope that he would be able to get a job from any of the debtors. His master commended him because he had at least used his wisdom to help the master collect some of his money. By helping his master, he also helped himself. Although he was dishonest, he used his dishonest method to his advantage. If he could do that, how much more, we that trust in God? We should be able to use God's means of prayer, faith, praise and worship to our advantage and to get our job. Instead of trying to combine little lies with God's methods, and think they will work, let us trust God whole-heartedly and employ his infallible means to get our job. God does not need your lies. Instead of trying to use part of the world's way and part of God's way to get your job, why not just use God's ways. The children of the world, work the world's system to get what they want, so why don't we too work God's ways to get our jobs?

The choice is yours, and the onus is on you.

CHAPTER 23

GETTING REFERENCES

*M*ost letters of employment for a job would normally have a clause stating that you have been offered the job subject to you fulfilling certain conditions. One of the most common conditions that is included is that you provide two or three people who they can contact for references. One could be from your present place of work, another from a previous employment, and the last could just be a character reference that you could get from a friend. If you've never worked, then they would most likely get references from your educational institution.

Most people have no issues finding someone to give them a reference, but some people struggle. This chapter is written for those who struggle to find someone to give them a reference.

There are many reasons why people struggle to find someone to give them a satisfactory reference. Some of the reasons can be due to the following:

- *Poor choices they made in the past*
- *Past mistakes*
- *Past failures*

- *Not getting along with a boss*
- *Being sacked from a job*
- *Not trusting your boss to give you a good reference*
- *Being misunderstood*
- *Not liked*
- *Bad credit (financial institutions and insurance companies could perform credit checks on you)*

This list is not exhaustive but what if you fall into this category of people? How will you overcome this hurdle? Can God help? Is this setback too complicated for God to handle?

Is anything too hard for God?

Do you remember the story of Daniel in the Lions' Den (*Daniel 6*)?

King Darius issued a decree that anyone who makes a petition to any God or man was to be thrown into the Lions' den. He did this based on the recommendation of most of his Advisers who were jealous of Daniel and wanted him killed. The King, unaware of their ploy, went ahead and passed the decree.

When the Advisers reported to the King that Daniel had broken the law and was to be punished, the King thought to himself, I must try to prevent Daniel from being thrown into the Lions' den because once he is thrown in, no one would be able to rescue him. The King did not realise that no situation is too hard for God and that no matter how difficult the situation is, God can still make a way where there is no way.

I believe that the King reasoned that the only way by which God would be able to deliver Daniel was if he could help God by preventing Daniel from being thrown into the Lions' den. How was God going to deliver Daniel from this situation with a predictable outcome - death? The King then tried to see if there was a loophole in the law which he could apply in order to help Daniel. But in as much as he tried and tried, he could not find one. The Advisers reminded the King that if he changed the law, he would be breaking the law of the Medes and Persians which clearly stated that no decree or statute which the King established could be changed.

To the natural man, this situation was a complex one. Was this situation really a hard one for God to handle?

The King laboured hard to rescue Daniel but he could not. He had to resign to the fact that Daniel had to be thrown into the Lions' den. Just before Daniel was thrown in, the King said to Daniel "Thy God whom thou serve continually will deliver you". Though he spoke words of comfort and reassurance, he spoke them out of fear and hope. He did not even have faith in the words that he spoke because he went to bed restless and could not even sleep because he was worried. He even had to pass the night fasting.

Eventually, Daniel was thrown in. Everything that could be done in the natural to ensure that Daniel was thrown in was done and a stone was brought and laid at the mouth of the den. Also, the King sealed it with his signet and that of the Lords; that the purpose might not be changed concerning Daniel.

Early in the morning, the King rose up and cried with a lamentable voice. "O Daniel, servant of the living God, Is thy God, whom thou serve continually, able to deliver you from the Lions? I don't think the King expected a reply but he was shocked when Daniel replied that God had sent his angel to shut the mouths of the Lions and that he was safe.

Though this situation was a difficult one, God was still able to deliver Daniel. It might have been a difficult and complex problem for man, but it was not a difficult one for God.

Is your job hunting situation a difficult one? Are you saying to yourself that God cannot solve this difficult situation? Daniel's situation was very complex. It was a foregone conclusion by everyone that once he was thrown in, he would not come out alive but he came out unscarred. No matter how complex your job situation is, God can handle it. The same God who was able to send his angel to shut the mouth of the Lions can make a way for you where there seems to be no way. Put your trust in him and watch him bring your deliverance. Remember, his thoughts are not our thoughts and his ways are not our ways (*Isaiah 55:8*).

Is anything too hard for God? No, nothing is too hard for God.

Personal Testimony

I was once made redundant from a job that I had worked in for 7 years, I was let go in late November and I thought to myself, "How am I going to get a job before Christmas?"

I kept sending out my C.V. Early in December, out of the blue, I got a call from a recruitment agent, he started chatting with me about a short contract job.

When I realised that it wasn't a bogus call, I started trying to sell myself so that he could at least put me forward for an interview. I was so surprised when he said "Can you start on Monday?"

I had not even been formally interviewed for the job, I had not seen the person I was to work with and I was being asked to start. Well, as I was in between jobs at that time, I accepted the offer.

When I dropped the phone, I said to myself, "Is that how to get a job?" I haven't been interviewed yet. You don't have to be interviewed before being offered a job. Nothing is too hard for God and God knows the Employers who are desperately looking for someone to start as soon as possible.

Romans 11:33 says that God's wisdom and knowledge are very deep and that it is difficult for us to comprehend his ways and methods. Let us always remember that though the situation might be hard for us, it is not a problem for God.

What do you do then?

The first thing to do is to make up your mind that you are not going to lie, do anything illegitimate, or compromise in anyway.

There is no use telling your friend to pose as your boss. God does not and will not have anything to do with lies. Remember that God can use whatever you have. There is no restraint on the Lord to save by many or by few.

Second, you need to pray to God to show you who to ask for a reference in your place of work. Ask the person for the reference and leave the rest to God.

Third, continue to look at the word. Do not take your eyes off the word of God. Remember that you have already received the job by faith.

Lastly, continue thanking God. *Ephesians 3:20* says, "*God is able to do exceeding and abundantly above all that we ask or think according to the power that works in us.*"

[8]For my thoughts are not your thoughts, neither are

your ways my ways, saith the LORD.
⁹For as the heavens are higher than the earth, so are my ways higher than your ways, and my thoughts than your thoughts.
¹⁰For as the rain cometh down, and the snow from heaven, and returneth not thither, but watereth the earth, and maketh it bring forth and bud, that it may give seed to the sower, and bread to the eater:
¹¹So shall my word be that goeth forth out of my mouth: it shall not return unto me void, but it shall accomplish that which I please, and it shall prosper in the thing whereto I sent it.

Isaiah 55:8–11

We need to believe and leave God to work it out the way he wants. Rest assured that God will fulfil his part of the bargain if you fulfil yours. Do not let fear, worry, or anxiety rob you of what is already yours.

God has already set before you an open door, and no man can shut it. Just fix your eyes on the word and watch God work wonders.

An example from the Bible

Incidentally, the Bible, in Genesis 39, has a record of someone who could potentially be deemed as having a bad reference. Despite this, they were still able to get an excellent job.

¹And Joseph was brought down to Egypt; and Potiphar, an officer of Pharaoh, captain of the guard, an Egyptian, bought him of the hands of the Ishmeelites, which had brought him down thither.

² And the Lord was with Joseph, and he was a prosperous man; and he was in the house of his master the Egyptian.

³ And his master saw that the Lord was with him, and that the Lord made all that he did to prosper in his hand.

⁴ And Joseph found grace in his sight, and he served him: and he made him overseer over his house, and all that he had he put into his hand.

⁵ And it came to pass from the time that he had made him overseer in his house, and over all that he had, that the Lord blessed the Egyptian's house for Joseph's sake; and the blessing of the Lord was upon all that he had in the house, and in the field.

⁶ And he left all that he had in Joseph's hand; and he knew not ought he had, save the bread which he did eat. And Joseph was a goodly person, and well favoured.

⁷ And it came to pass after these things, that his master's wife cast her eyes upon Joseph; and she said, Lie with me.

⁸ But he refused, and said unto his master's wife, Behold, my master wotteth not what is with me in the house, and he hath committed all that he hath to my hand;

⁹ There is none greater in this house than I; neither hath he kept back any thing from me but thee, because thou art his wife: how then can I do this great wickedness, and sin against God?

¹⁰ And it came to pass, as she spake to Joseph day by day, that he hearkened not unto her, to lie by her, or to be with her.

¹¹ And it came to pass about this time, that Joseph went into the house to do his business; and there was none of the men of the house there within.

¹² And she caught him by his garment, saying, Lie with

me: and he left his garment in her hand, and fled, and got him out.

¹³ *And it came to pass, when she saw that he had left his garment in her hand, and was fled forth,*

¹⁴ *That she called unto the men of her house, and spake unto them, saying, See, he hath brought in an Hebrew unto us to mock us; he came in unto me to lie with me, and I cried with a loud voice:*

¹⁵ *And it came to pass, when he heard that I lifted up my voice and cried, that he left his garment with me, and fled, and got him out.*

¹⁶ *And she laid up his garment by her, until his lord came home.*

¹⁷ *And she spake unto him according to these words, saying, The Hebrew servant, which thou hast brought unto us, came in unto me to mock me:*

¹⁸ *And it came to pass, as I lifted up my voice and cried, that he left his garment with me, and fled out.*

¹⁹ *And it came to pass, when his master heard the words of his wife, which she spake unto him, saying, After this manner did thy servant to me; that his wrath was kindled.*

²⁰ *And Joseph's master took him, and put him into the prison, a place where the king's prisoners were bound: and he was there in the prison.*

²¹ *But the Lord was with Joseph, and shewed him mercy, and gave him favour in the sight of the keeper of the prison..*

Genesis 39:1-21

Joseph was in prison, and although he did not actually commit the offense for which he was accused, there was evidence to prove that he had done it. There was no logical way of exonerating himself. All fingers were pointing to the fact that he had actually committed the deed.

Despite this setback, Joseph was able to get a job as the Prime Minister. How did God bypass the negative situation which had tarnished his good name? It was never an issue for God and his imprisonment was not brought up because he solved an uncommon problem. He was able to get a job that only people without any taint to their character would have got. The Bible makes us understand that God was with Joseph and the God factor in this life made room for him.

The amazing thing about this story was that the King knew that he was a prisoner. The King needed to solve the problem so much so that, he did not care if the person had a bad history or not. He was so desperate that the bad history was irrelevant in the selection process. What mattered to the King was that the spirit of God was in him and helped him solve an impossible problem that others could not solve.

God can make your prospective employer focus on the fact that you are the answer to their problem instead of focusing on your negative employment history. You too, will need to focus on God instead of your past flaws. Keep your eyes on the one helping you (God) instead of any negative occurrence that you have previously experienced. God is a God of a second chance and will make a way for you where there seems to be no way. God is bigger than your past mistakes.

I experienced something like that in the past. I worked in a company in the heart of London. When my immediate boss was relocated to another country, the boss who took over from him did not like me. He was very hostile to me and did not hide this hostility. Different uncomfortable things were happening at work, and I decided to give in my notice and resign. I had a three month notice period to look for another job. One of the thoughts that nagged me was how I was going to get a reference from this boss. I did not want to ask him because I did not think it was appropriate to ask someone who openly detested me for a reference.

I prayed about it, and God led me to ask someone else in the company. The person who God led me to, was also not a perfect person, and I did not really trust him. But I went on with the leading and asked him for a reference. I don't really know what he wrote, but I successfully passed the screening process.

I subsequently encountered this reference issue again with the last company I worked for in the UK before I left for Canada. It was a contract role. I worked really hard and had a good working relationship with my boss. However, I did not disclose the fact that I was planning to move to Canada to anyone despite having had many opportunities to do so. When it came to the time for them to renew my contract, I told them that I was not interested in the renewal because I was relocating to Canada. This might have offended my boss because I had many opportunities to tell him that I was leaving. When I got to Canada, I emailed him a number of times, but he did not respond to my emails. I knew then that I could not ask him to give me a reference. It bothered me, and I kept wandering who I would ask to give me a reference. I had worked closely with him, and he naturally seemed like the most reasonable person to ask. I decided that I would cross that bridge when I got to it.

When I was finally offered a job in Canada, I was surprised that I was not asked for a reference. At first, I thought it was an oversight, but it was later that I realised that the company had a policy of observing you for the first three months and then getting rid of you if you were not up to scratch.

I am saying all this, to say that, God is a God of a second chance and can get you past any hurdle in the screening process.

CHAPTER 24

KEEP YOUR JOB BY FAITH

³Are ye so foolish? having begun in the Spirit, are ye now made perfect by the flesh?

Galatians 3:3

*W*hat we began in the spirit must also be completed in the spirit. Although this book is about getting a job, I want to go over the topic of keeping your job by faith.

God has miraculously granted you the desires of your heart. You have received your offer letter and fulfilled all conditions. You have been told when to resume work at your office. What should you do now?

I do not want to be the bearer of bad news, but you need to remember that you fought the good fight of faith and won against the devil. So, it goes without saying that he will be mad that you got your job. You won the battle against him by faith, so you need to keep your job by faith.

The good news is that when God blesses you, no one can curse you *(Numbers 23:8)*.

There are many things the people of this world do to keep their jobs. You are not going to keep your job by faith if you engage in such tactics.

The world thinks that to keep your job, you need to do the following:

- *Work unimaginable hours*
- *Lie to your bosses*
- *Lie about a colleague*
- *Put down someone who is better than you*
- *Cheat*
- *Flirt with your bosses*
- *Act immorally*
- *Backstab your colleagues*
- *Exaggerate your accomplishments*
- *Pretend to have common interests as your bosses*
- *Act dishonestly to protect their jobs*
- *Participate in office politics to enhance your promotion prospects*

What does the Bible say about conducting ourselves in the workplace? And what do we need to do to keep our jobs by faith?

- *Put God first and trust him (Exodus 20:3; Proverbs 29:25)*
- *Acknowledge God in everything (Proverbs 3:6)*
- *Always give God the glory (Colossians 3:17)*
- *Never take God's glory (Isaiah 42:8)*
- *Be approachable (Proverbs 18:24)*
- *Be willing to help others (Luke 10:27)*
- *Get to work on time (Proverbs 6:9)*
- *Be diligent in your work (Proverbs 22:29)*

- *Pay attention to detail (Hebrews 2:1)*
- *Update your skills (Proverbs 12:24)*
- *Do not be lazy (Proverbs 6:6)*
- *Keep up with the latest technology (Proverbs 21:5)*
- *Invest your own personal time in bringing your skills up to date (Proverbs 14:23)*
- *Do not carry out your own personal business during office hours (Colossians 3:23)*
- *Do not use the office phone for your own personal business.(Luke 16:12)*
- *Do not use your time at work for your own personal matters (Luke 16:12)*
- *Be pro-active (Proverbs 6:6–9)*
- *Be willing to put in extra time without asking for overtime pay (Matthew 5:41)*
- *Be willing to do the job others are not willing to do (Galatians 6:7–9)*
- *Be faithful (2 Timothy 2:1–2; Luke 16:10)*
- *Be dependable (1 Corinthians 4:2)*
- *Do not be a people-pleaser but be a God-pleaser (Ephesians 6:6; Galatians 1:10; John 12:43)*
- *Do not hold grudges and forgive those that have offended you (Ephesians 4:31–32)*
- *Overlook faults (Romans 12:17–21)*
- *Do not backbite (Proverbs 11:13)*
- *Do not lie. Admit any fault or wrongdoing (Colossians 3:9–10)*

The above list is not exhaustive, and we need to remember that people are always watching us.

Remember the story of Joseph when he was in Potiphar's house. He was promoted because he stood out. This same Joseph was also put in charge when he got thrown into prison. Joseph had some qualities that we need to emulate in our jobs.

Even when nobody was watching, Joseph purposed in his heart to do good.

One thing that stood out to me most about the life of Joseph was when Potiphar's wife kept asking him to lie with her (*Genesis 39:7*). Joseph refused. He said, "*How then can I do this great wickedness and sin against God?*" What puzzled me here was that he did not think he would be sinning against Potiphar but against God. Surely, it was Potiphar's wife that he was going to sleep with. One would have thought the sin would have been against Potiphar, but Joseph said it would be a sin against God. Joseph was indeed a God-pleaser and not a man-pleaser because he did everything to please God and not man.

Joseph did the right thing even when no one was watching. If Joseph had slept with Potiphar's wife when no one else was present, no one would have known. But Joseph chose to do the right thing even when nobody else was there.

Joseph was hardworking, trustworthy, and

diligent. Consequently, he was always promoted wherever he went. He always stood out. He always went the extra mile and gave everything his best shot. He was not looking for ways to cut corners or leave the job for someone else to do. He did his job as if he did it unto God and not to man. Hence, he always glorified God in his job.

He forgave his brothers when they sold him to slavery and was willing to help them when they came to Egypt to buy food. He did not repay evil for evil but left it to God to dish out the revenge to his offenders.

He stood out in the eyes of men and God, and he was promoted to the job that most people would have died for.

Now that you've got this job by faith, you must keep it by faith and glorify God.

In conclusion, there is nothing too hard for God. God will grant you the desires of your heart if you seek and trust him wholeheartedly for that job.

MY CONFESSION FOR MY JOB

Father, I thank you because *Mark 11:23* says I should believe I receive when I pray.

I believe I received my job when I prayed and I thank you for it. (*2 Corinthians 5:7*)

I walk by faith and not by sight and I refuse to be moved by my five senses.

I trust in you with all my heart and I do not rely on my understanding. (*Proverbs 3:5-6*)

Every situation, circumstance, evidence or experience that does not align with your word is not the truth. Your word is the truth and it will come to pass in my life.

I will not waver, doubt or worry.

I will not fear or be anxious.

I will not give room to the lies of the enemy.

Thank you Lord because I believe I have my job.

www.ingramcontent.com/pod-product-compliance
Lightning Source LLC
Chambersburg PA
CBHW020855090426
42736CB00008B/377